DIALECTICS OF FREEDOM IN SOMERSET MAUGHAM

DIALECTICS OF FREEDOM IN SOMERSET MAUGHAM

Adibur Rahman

Publications

KALPAZ PUBLICATIONS

DELHI-110 052

Dialectics of Freedom in Somerset Maugham

Rs. 690

ISBN : 81-7835-447-0

Published in 2005 in India by
Kalpaz Publications
C-30, Satyawati Nagar
Delhi-110 052
Email : kalpaz@hotmail.com

Lasertype Setting by: Tact Computer Graphics, Delhi
Printed at: Salasar Imaging System, Delhi

Contents

Preface

Somerset Maugham's flair of writing naturalises all those scientific, mechanical and evolutionary processes Man has undergone in his bid to achieve emancipation from the centuries long suffering. Maugham with all his insight and clairvoyance dialectically envisages that the colossal growth of the scientific facts proved itself to be a pathetic fallacy. Maugham was a disillusioned realist who through his empathy could vividly see that the instrument of realism was no more feasible for projecting the whole panorama of man in the post modern era and that art had to be liberated from the cult of the realistic writing. With the emergence of the neo-industrial and mechanical society, there cropped up a ghastly civilization; the 'new' man emanated from the collocations of the scientific facts, says Maugham, feels himself alien in a society which no more caters to the aesthetic needs of the throbbing 'self'. As Maugham is an existentialist, he bifurcates between 'essence' and existence.

Born (1874-1965) into the confines of conventional society which had proclivity to stifle aspirations of the self enkindled in him an urge to create a world in which there would be a complete harmony between his 'self' and environs. The conventional ethics as Maugham saw was spiritually dysfunctional. The 'new' man looking up for a way out to emerge from the life of bondage aesthetically aspired for attaining self-fulfilment. Maugham is a writer who can be placed in the dialectical tradition by virtue of which he could see how man remains caught up in the self-illusory life of the 'real' world. He is an optimist who dialectically believes in the gospel of the apocalypse. He emphatically makes assertion of his stance of life saying that Man in the mechanically metamorphosed social scenario, has been made servile to mechanical society, need not be bemused and annihilited; instead he optimistically delineates the dialectics of freedom which, to him, alone could take man to self realization, fulfilment and above all to the road of freedom.

Marx and Engels, on the one hand saw redemption in Dialectical Materialism. Dialectical Materialism says Maugham had nothing to do with the ingrained ethical, mystical and metaphysical realizations. Man says Maugham is not a product of his being; rather Man is what he experiences to be. In Maugham's Dialectics of freedom there could be a real attainment of freedom and self-fulfilment if Man applies the dynamics of dialectical perspective. Freedom to him is not limited to the 'algebra of infinities' and to mere attainment of happiness in the real and the materialistic society. In fact what Maugham is after is evolving a larger reality to brace up and intermingle both the ethical and aesthetic realizations of the human existence on the dialectical plane. To identify Maugham to be a mere writer in the Naturalistic tradition, is to miss the dialectical art which he applies to retrieve art from the pretensions and hypocrisies of the cult of realism. In 'Cakes and Ale' Maugham basically applies the 'naturalistic art' to dismantle the social barriers which lie barricaded between 'us' and 'they'. His 'Cakes and Ale' which has been written in the first person narration, shows up Maugham's aversion to all those man-made social barriers that entwine man into the self-illusory life of the 'real' world; Maugham naturalistically writes "I do not know that the people I lived among were pretentious in the sense of making themselves out to be richer or grander than they really were, but looking back it does seem to me that they lived a life full of pretences. They dwelt behind a mask of respectability".

Playing the role of a literary critic, Maugham, hence, comes to realize that art had to be liberated from the realistic cult of writing. Like Flaubert, Maugham too believes that art has a meaningful role to play in cohering the inertia of the self with the 'real' world. In his remarkable essay The 'Writer's point of view' he clearly writes that 'the aim of the writer of fiction. I repeat is not to instruct but to please.' What is striking is that Maugham unflinchingly concentrates on the inertia of the 'self'. Maugham writes; 'I am only conscious to know what is in me that is disagreeable to them'. In "The Moon and Six Pence", he portrays the picture of an artist who sacrifices everything he owes—family home and reputation for the sake of art, Maugham writes; "Art is a manifestation of emotion, and emotion speaks a language that all may understand. But I would allow that the critic who has not a practical knowledge of technique is seldom able to say anything on the subject to real value, and my ignorance of painting is extreme". It can however be logically argued that there is a relation between art and consciousness. It is the consciousness which through the vehicle of art manifests itself. Maugham writes; "The moral I draw is that the writer should seek his reward in the pleasure of his work and in release from the burden of his thoughts; and, indifferent to aught else, nothing for praise or censure, failure or success." Being conscious of the inadequacies of the realistic cult of writing Maugham coheres both the ethical and aesthetic aspects of life in order to bring into focus a fuller perspective of human life. Maugham at the same time shows his commitment to moral stories in 'rhymed couplets', he ethically writes; "I will continue to write moral stories in rhymed couplets. But I should thrice of a fool if I did it for aught but my own entertainment".

Maugham like Spinoza regards good and evil as self-illusory; he in the same vein practically applies the implied objectivity in his understanding of Man and his environs.

Maugham knows no cynicism by exploring those dark, elemental savage passions. He dialectically intends to make man conscious of the fury of passions; He aesthtically argues that the aesthetic emotion of multitudes shape up the magnitude of the third dimensions. He opines that the implied, subliminal and stark savage passions are themselves a larger reality. Maugham, at the same time points out at the limitations of the colossal growth of scientific facts which lack pespicacity of taking into account the ethical and aesthetic aspects of life. Unlike Eliot Maugham aesthetically argues that the emotion of multitudes and the subliminal stark passions equally play a pivotal ole in making man conscious of the 'the new side of the self'.

G.B. Shaw, on the one hand was a disillusioned romancticist; Maugham on the other hand, was a disillusioned realist. Maugham's of Human Bondage and The Razer's Edge in identical ways, explore man's innate urge to define his self in the outside world. Maugham in his varied novels, essays and stories basically writes how Man feels his 'self' alien in the 'real' world. Thus, from the dialectical standpoint the 'real' becomes self-illusory. In both his remarkable novels 'of human bondage' and 'The Razor's Edge' Man has been shown frantically running after the self-illusory life which ironically end up with the 'algebra of infinities'. Maugham is a literary critic who is of the view that realism is no more relevant to explore the 'ambiguities' which the colossal growth of science has cropped up in the post modern era. Maugham applies the mechanics of the 'dialectical art to fill up those ambiguities of the collocations of atoms with the aesthetic emotion. Maugham's art of fiction is thus based upon the doctrine of the inner self. The characters projected on Maugham's dialectical canvas, have no way out but to rebel against the conventional ethics and scramble for freedom from the self illusory life of the post modern society. In 'Of Human Bondage' and 'The Razor's Edge' Man has ironically been shown hankering after the self-illusory life. Arundhati Roy regards the endless materialistic pursuit of life as algebra of infinities. Maugham dialectically connotates that realism is no more an answer to man's dream of attaining fuller realizations of his aesthetic 'being'. Maugham neither believes in the Wellsyan concept of the scientific paradise. Nor does he believe in dialectical materialism on which man had raised his hope of redemption, proved itself to be 'unreal' and flimsy. What Maugham aesthetically aspires for is to make Man conscious of the mettle man is made up of. The basic instincts which remain implicit within the 'self' seek participation in every stance of defining the aesthetic emotion. The conflict taking place between the self-illusory and the aesthetic values is the vehicle on which Maugham's characters move up for attaining emancipation on the dialectical plane. Thus the urge to get emancipated from the life of bondage gives impetus to the characters he portrays. In 'Of Human Bondage' Maugham shows his anxiety at the colossal growth of science. The basic problems which Maugham faces is how to deal with the evolutionary and scientific processes in the correct perspective. Thus he dialectically wants to make science religion and religion science. The ignominy faced by man in the post modern era wherein the colossal growth of scientific facts tend to subdue and stifle the subliminal emotions while seeking participation in every stance Man puts up in the 'real' world. In his another novel, 'The Magician' the perversity of the evil has been shown in the garb of the camouflage. Hado's hedonistic, sinister and diabolical designs show how Man finds himself belittled and metamorphosed in his defiance against the devil incarnate. In 'The Summing Up' Maugham plays the role of a literary critic. He is basically of the view that art can't afford to play a subservient role in its exploration of the 'real' and spiritually hollow mundane society. In 'The Painted Veil' Maugham envisages a world beyond multiculturalism in which 'love' and 'duty' remain ensconced with each other; 'The Razor's Edge' is an ardent quest for emancipation on the aesthetic, metaphysical and mystical planes. Maugham dialectically says that man can't attain emancipation unless he concentrates on the inertia of the self. The consciousness implicit in him creates a faculty of rationalistically understanding the environs he dwells in. In both the novels, Maugham shows his anxiety at the way the conventional ethics makes abstract morality dysfunctional and inoperative. Maugham with all his insight and clairvoyance could see the hypocrisies and pretences of the spiritually hollow society which is fed merely on the scientific facts, no longer cater to the aesthetic aspirations of the self. In his novel, 'The Magician' Maugham strips off the 'painted' veil of the 'real' world in which indwells the deep-seated evil and its maglinancy. 'Beauty', says he, can't be taken merely on the literal plane; 'Beauty' instead has ethical function to ennoble man for better understanding of man and his environs. Maugham doesn't take beauty merely on the literal plane instead the beauty he explicates is an extended metaphor of his adherence to the ethical, apocalyptical, mystical and above all to the artistic manifestation of life. It is the ethical explication of beauty on which Maugham draws a line of demarcation between sacred and the profane.

Acknowledgements

I feel great pleasure in expressing my gratitude to my teacher, Dr. Iven Masih, University Professor of English, Magadh University, Bodh Gaya for enkindling in me a creative urge to work enthusiastically. His love and companionship will go on to enthral me in my facing the adversities of life. I convey my best regards to him for his ardent sincerity and kindness which he bestowed upon me.

I am grateful to Dr. R.K. Gupta, Editor-in Chief, Atlantic Publishers, New Delhi for publishing my book on George Orwell.

I convey my best regards to Dr. Gupteshwar Prasad, D. Litt. and (Retd.) University Professor of English, Gaya College Gaya, M.U. Who always inspired me with his kindness and learning. I also extend my thanks to my friend, Priye Ranjan Dwayr who advised me to get the present book published under the script of Kalpaz Publications. I convey my thanks to my brother, M.N. Rahman who always supported me in difficult times.

Finally I express my heartfelt floral tributes to my grandfather, Late Abdul Baqui whose generosity is still a source of inspiration for me.

Adibur Rahman

Introduction

Somerset Maugham (1874-1965) is a post - war British novelist. With the emergence of the neo-meachanical order Maugham dialectically searches for new avenues of freedom. The suppression wreaked up by the man-made social constraints, says Maugham impedes emancipation of man. He breaks new grounds for attainment of freedom in which man can define his self in the neo-meachnical society. As Shaw is a disillusioned romanticist, Maugham on the other hand, is a disillusioned realist who dialectically discerns that realism in is no more answer to the problems emanating from the post modern society. Shaw saw that root cause of human suffering lay in economic deprivation. Maugham instead says that the deep dungeons of poverty are themselves a part of the human consciousness. In his various writing, novels, stories and essays, he emphatically argues that experience too can become a stepping-stone of spritulsing the senses. Man says Maugham need not be bemused at the colossal growth of the scientific progress. In Of Human Bondage (1915) the metaphysics of love is realised in denying the attainment of happiness. Like D.H. Lawrence Maugham revels in unfolding the primitive, dark savage passions which in 'full throated ease', hold man in bondage. Maugham like Spinoza regards both good and evil as self-illusory. He elaborates his concept of casuistry—the applied ethics showing his aversion to the dysfunctional morality. In The Moon and Six Pence, Maugham aesthetically shows how the dark savage passions inculcate man in bondage. Unlike Jonathan swift, Maugham knows no cynicism. By exploring those dark, elemental passions he dialectically intends to make man conscious of the fury of passions. Maugham thus eloquently argues that the aesthetic emotion of multitudes shapes up and creates the magnitude of the third dimensions. Elaborating his dialectical consciousness Maugham says that the implicit, subliminal and stark passions are themselves a greater reality seeking participation in every externality of human behaviour.

Maugham at the same time points out at limitations of the colossal growth of the scientific facts, which lack perspicacity in taking into account the ethical and aesthetic aspects of human life. Disagreeing with T.S. Eliot, Maugham aesthetically argues that the emotion of multitudes; the subliminal and stark passions equally play a pivotal role in making Man conscious of the 'new side of the self'. Nor does Maugham agree to Eliot's 'turning loose of emotions' and 'extinction of personality'. The 'aesthetic emotion' in Maugham's exploration of art enkindles an urge to define all his aesthetic and instinctual patterns in the 'real world'. Maugham thus applies the art of making the subjective objective for creating a larger reality.

Maugham is aesthetically conscious that love sought in terms of consummation embroils man in the endless annals of loneliness. Maugham is a literary critic who could envision and see that realism was no more relevant to address the 'ambiguities', which the enormous growth of science has cropped up in the post-modern era. Maugham applies the mechanics of the dialectical art to fill up those ambiguities of the collocations of atoms with the aesthetic emotion in order to achieve self-fulfillment.

Maugham's art is based upon the doctrine of the innerself. The doctrine of the innerself says Maugham, is the inbuilt vehicle, which gives impetus to man in defining the stance of the self. In The painted veil (1925) Maugham envisages a world beyond multi-culturisim in which 'love' and 'duty' remain ensconced with each other. In Of Human Bondage and 'The Razor's Edge' the metaphysics of love has been perceived in denying happiness sought in the rationalistic terms. In both the novels man has been shown caught up in the web of the illusive life. The quest of freedom in Maugham's realm of fiction can't be turned into a concrete reality unless man concentrates inertia of the self. Maugham shows his anxiety at the way the conventional ethics makes abstract morality dysfunctional and inoperative. Maugham with his applicability of dialectical art, magic and clairvoyance could see that the post-modern society which is fed merely on the scientific facts, no longer caters to the aesthetic aspirations of the self. Maugham thus gives supreme importance to the survival of the individual. In Cakes and Ale (1930) Maugham aspires for bridging up the gaps between 'us' and 'they'. In his remarkable works like Cakes and Ale and The Summing up (1939) Maugham emerges on the literary horizon as a literary critic of great repute. Liza of Lambeth (1897) is one of his early novel, which brought him to limelight, and reputation giving him impetus to write great novels like Of Human Bondage and The Razor's Edge.

Maugham had a little faith in the altruistic measures taken up by man. The basic fact which

Maugham discerns is all Man's altruistic measures to achieve happiness sought in the 'real' world is something akin to Man's running after the illusive life. The humanists like Shaw, Galsworthy and Wells were all for diminution of human suffering by applying the humanistic, scientific, economic and intellectual aspects of human life. What they miss to project is the voice of the inner self that essentially provides sanity to each and every stance a human being takes in his life. Nor does Maugham agree with Bennet's exploration of the pacifistic panorama of life in which Man has been shown deeply steeped in resignation and acceptance of stoic life. In his novels like 'Clayhanger' and 'Old Wives' Tales', Bennet revels in portraying a panorama of life in which characters are pitted against stoic way of life. Maugham, who was well aware of the mechanics of the doctrine of the inner self, firmly believed that the pursuit of happiness in the 'real' world leads to splitting up of personality. Maugham's dialectical approach thus puts emphasis on making the invisible visible.

H.G. Well's scientific romance on the one hand, has given rise to the concept of Utopia. All Wells' aspirations of achieving emancipation by dint of the enormous growth of science and intellect rationalistically aim at attaining satisfaction. Maugham on the other hand, opines that life can't be made meaningful unless the inoperative conventional morality is made operative on the dialectical plane. Maugham in his various novels and other writings dialectically believes that 'experience' too can spiritualize the 'senses'. Ruskin on the contrary, says that 'senses' are an obstacle to the feeling of the 'beautiful'. Explicating his concept of morality Ruskin opines that it is the feeling of the beautiful which depends on intellect, gratitude and joy. W.H Auden and Stephen Spender who belonged to the Thirties saw art and beauty in their proclivity to the Left orthodoxy. Shaw in an identical way applies his theory of life for creating a better generation. The conflict in the Shavian philosophy operates between illusion and reality. Both Wells and Shaw ironically came to see that the rationalistic and scientific approach to life would open floodgates for ameliorating the impoverished masses. Shaw takes anti-romantic stance while dealing with the problems that exist on the real plane. Walter Pater too pronounces that art can no longer play a subservient role. Art from Croce's concept is intuition or expression of an impression within the substance of the human mind. The intuitive processes working within the mind receive millions of impulses. The impression coming on to the compass of those impulses receives the tint of imagination making the impression expression. In principles of criticism I.A. Richards interprets relation between criticism and science. In his opinion, the human psychology has lot to do with the principles of literary criticism. Maugham presents a panorama of life, which moves about the spur of the doctrine of the inner self. The canvas he paints is a panorama of life which presents too much of the knowledge of the self. The more man knows of the interior monologues, says Freud, the more he knows of the growing consciousness of his inner personality. The human mind says, Richards, is a system of impulses. Each new experience brings communication to the impulses. The substance of the human mind remains static unless it gets itself readjusted with the new impulses. The mind aims at deriving maximum impulses. Richards further reiterates how the play of impulses enhances the area of the experience.

Elaborating how the psychic processes shape up literary criticism, Richards like Croce and Coleridge, bifurcates nature of experience into appetencies and desires. Mangham's characters are too much conscious of the self, as well as of the aesthetic and instinctual patterns of life. Being conscious of the mettle of the self, his characters know no escape from the aesthetic and instinctual aspects of the human life, which remain invisible to the 'real' world while they remain at play.

Maugham's 'Of Human bondage' is not an autobiography but an autobiographical novel projected on the miniature of his canvas. Philip is made to play the role of an objective observer. His proceedings of his childhood days, his adolescence and adulthood are replete with an impartial and objective vision. He has been projected to replay the reminiscences that haunt him throughout his life. He defines his self in a society, which is essentially hostile. Philip as a boy faces the onslaught of the conventional morality is indicative of the basic fact how Maugham's childhood had been at loggerheads with the conventional morality. Unlike Freud, Maugham is of the view that the psycho-analytical method alone can't depict true behavioural patterns of the modern life. Like Freud, Richards too says that the mind undergoes a process of selection and rejection on the basis of the impulses that move up the mind. The selection of the interior monologues taking place within the psyche, says Freud, constitutes the consciousness of the human mind. Likewise Richards reiterates that the faculty of reasoning operating within the Psyche either selects appetencies or rejects aversions. Maugham on the other hand, places his characters on the pedestal of his canvas exploring the area and compass of the human consciousness in miniature. Maugham's projection of the canvas is limited but amplified in the sense that his characters always come up to the outside 'real' world in the light of consciousness they carry from within. It is in the sense that his characters act in miniature. They incessantly ratiocinate the inherent appetencies and aversions on the basis of which they differentiate between the sacred and the profane; good and evil.; beautiful and ugly. They can go either of the two perspectives, which move up and accelerate the spur of the doctrine of the inner self. Unlike Graham Greene and Eveylyn Waugh, Maugham does not repose his faith in the catholic dogmas. Maugham's characters revel and bask in glory to put up the stance of life in a bid to seek emancipation from the conventional ethics. In Of Human Bondage, emancipation of man has neither been sought in the scientific Utopia nor in the psycho-analytical method instead greater emancipation can be aesthetically realized by the spiritualizing the ever-growing web of the scientific facts. The scientific facts intermingled with fiction, says Maugham can play a vital role for bringing about greater emancipation for man on the planet earth. Maugham in, Of Human Bondage, brings into focus all those instinctual patterns, which get evocative in every human relationship. Philip can't ignore those aesthetic aspirations. He goes on to pass from one human relationship to another, Fanny Price, Hayward, Isabel, Kitty and Mildred all move up onto Maugham's canvas of the fictional art. Each and every character, which Maugham creates, seeks emancipation from the life of bondage in his own way. Their implicit proclivity to yield to passion is something what constitutes human bondage. Thus, Maugham's characters move up anticlockwise. By going beyond the life of Americanism, Larry lives against the streams of the conventional society. Happiness sought in terms of the scientific and rationalistic processes would push him to the brink of isolation and loss of identity. Denial of happiness, the happiness that would take him to seek satisfaction out of living a life of Americanism, would embroil him in illusion. Maugham's art of fiction thus breaks new ground for catering to ethical and aesthetic aspirations of Man. Larry wants to do 'nothing' and Liza is seized up with exhilarating sensation of getting emancipated from the life of bondage. Julia is entrapped in and tied to the theatre of the absurd in which deriving satisfaction on the physical and rationalistic planes are given supreme importance. The need to cater to her aesthetic aspirations creates in her a new woman for seeking real emancipation and security. For Maugham the scientific paradise devoid of the participation of the 'self leads to spiritual sterility and splitting up of personality It is in this sense that the pursuit of happiness in the 'real' world is nothing but self-illusory. The world, which Maugham depicts, projects man at loggerheads with the alien society. Man in the face of feeling his 'self stifled in the alien and hostile society, scrambles for freedom from the illusive life that holds him in bondage. Maugham dialectically aspires for greater emancipation from the life of bondage and impoverishment. Thus, the aesthetic emotions of multitude which lies deep-seated in man themselves, has a being of their own, needs to be dialectically addressed. The colossal growth of science projected for bringing about happiness on the mere intellectual, economic and rationalistic planes, would not be feasible in the modern context.

P. B. Shelley in, Prometheus Unbound, explores the myth of suffering. Shelly mythologically explores the agony and anguish of being enchained into the irretrievable knots of suffering. In the Orwellian fantasy, the individual in Man has been shown declining to conform to the ethics of the collectivist society. In Orwell's' Animal Farm' and 'Nineteen Eighty Four', his protagonists have been shown struggling against the onslaught of the state control in which all human aspirations of coming up the cult of totalitarianism—constitutes a different pitch of human bondage and loneliness. In Maugham's exploration of human bondage it is the stark savage passions, which hold Man in bondage. Strickland, Philip, Liza, Larry and Kitty each and every character Maugham creates on his canvas of fictional art, yields to sublime and elemental passions. Thus, Maugham's characters have tenacity to unentwine themselves from the bondage, which sharpens their voice of dissent. It can therefore be rationalistically argued that Maugham's characters are true to the Promethean spirit. Irrespective of the suffering they receive while facing the odds, it is their endeavor of getting emancipation from conventional morality, which matters most to them. Liza who is moved up with her frenzy of coming up limitations of the mundane life is ironically unconscious of the mettle of her self. Her yielding to passion embroils her in a life of bondage. Jim's Jarring notes of libido lasciviously entwine her into the tentacles of uninhibited suffering. Julia too, in an identical way was unconscious of the longing of her self before she is tied to matrimony. For Michael she is nothing but an object of desire. Her passion for displaying her theatrical skills as well as for attaining the theatrical glamour basically strikes her from within which no more gives thrill and sensation. Her aesthetic awakening thus gives rise to a 'new' woman; she is something like a phoenix rising out of her own ashes. Thus, each and each every character Maugham portrays, even Sophie who succumbs to drink and a violent death, get what they aspire for. Fanny Price in Of Human Bondage, too in an identical way perishes while living in Paris. Rosie in 'Cakes and Ale', is a character built up upon the cult of Naturalism, lives a life of fun and frolics. Strickland in 'The Moon and Six Pence' forsakes his life of happiness. Yielding to aversion; he goes away to forlorn and desolatory landscapes of Tahiti to see motley colours of the inner self in all its shades and designs.

Maugham's quest for art, beauty, magic and clairvoyance is no less significant than his moral preponderance. He is equally critical of the 'new' world, which is alien-to the instinctual and aesthetic aspirations of the 'self. Maugham's fiction thus opens up a new horizon in which Man's aesthetic life needs to be dialectically addressed. Maugham in 'The Razor's Edge' syllogistically elaborates the Paradox of evil. Evil, says Maugham, is a direct manifestation of the divine good. Like E.M. Forster he comes to realize that both good and evil remain sacrosanct to each other, as they are manifest in human nature. 'When evil recedes, says Forster, good becomes explicit. In his numerous novels what Maugham dialectically argues is that the colossal growth of science and technology in the 'real' world is just one side of the spur; it can be made operative only when fillip side of the aesthetic and the instinctual patterns of human life is braced up with. Maugham stands closer to the modern novelists and dialectically discerns how the Paradox of eternal hierarchy, entwines Man is bondage. Maugham's Naturalism thus naturalizes all those scientific, mechanical and evolutionary progresses man has ever made in a bid to emancipate him from the centuries long bondage.

Maugham aesthetically explores the various facets of human relationships prevailing in the 'real' world. Flaubert says that it is hatred of 'realism' that made him undertake writing novels in the Naturalistic tradition. The inoperative realistic cult of writing says he, is no more relevant to project man with all his motley colours of the self. Maugham's exploration of human relationship is different from those of his contemporary writers. It is the illusory self of man that makes him believe he materialistically achieves satiety on the rationalistic plane. He temporarily enjoys freedom, economic prosperity and security but after gradual unfolding of the absolute he comes to realize that all his hankering after the materialistic pursuit of life is mere perfunctory. Maugham doesn't believe in the Epicurean dictum that—ripeness is all. The need to innovate a new lease of life thus provides Maugham the basic impetus to define his self in the spiritually sterile 'real' world. Though Maugham's characters scramble to get retrieved from suffering heaped up on them by the mechanistic society yet the urge to be emancipated from the life of bondage enkindles in him a new lease of life. The dream of getting emancipated from onslaught of the 'real' world goes on to remain a distant dream. Self-fulfillment is thus a driving force while keeping up Maugham's characters moving from one human predicament to another. Being a disillusioned realist Maugham looks at the bizarre bazaar of the 'real' world in which man is caught up into the web of his illusive life. As 'wants are unlimited', search for happiness merely on the economic and rationalistic planes would not be feasible. A materialistic pursuit of life in the realistic society says Maugham merely stifles and annihilates human aspirations of attainting freedom. In 'Point Counter

Point', Aldous Huxley delineates his search for freedom in a society in which vitality of human relationship is dwindling fast. In his various novels like point counter Point, Brawe New World and Barren Leaves, he interprets the spiritual sickness of the dangers living in the scientific paradise. In his novel, Island, Huxley aspires for a society in which sanity and flamboyance of vitality have been dreamt of. Both Huxley and Lawrence in identical ways, lament at loss of verbiage and vitality of the modern wasteland. 'April' no more creates spiritual awakening in Eliot's 'The Waste Land'. Duality of voice in Eliot's "The Love Song of Alfred J Pruforck' can be realistically felt. 'Let us you and I' is indicative of the basic fact how the colossal growth of science leads to the splitting up of personality. In Eliot's 'Portrait of the Lady', the woman with her lingering fear of alienation makes all out effort to tempt the protagonist. She frantically reiterates him to live a life of pleasure, which ends with a fuss. Eliot realistically explores the modern phenomena like indecision, dilemma and conflict taking place into the psyche of the modern man. In Eliot's 'Ash Wednesday' the modern man resolves to live a life of resignation and surrender. Thus, emancipation from Eliot's standpoint lies in not yielding to the ethics of the spiritually hollow realistic society. The images employed in Eliot's 'Ash Wednesday' evoke in man a resolution not to yield to the spiritually hollow 'real' world. In 'Hollow Men', 'Gerontion' and The Wasteland, the anguish of living in the 'unreal', flimsy and artificial life bring into focus the nature of the human predicament in the modern society.

Maugham is dialectically conscious of the dichotomy of the self and the annihilating effects of the enormity of intellect. Yeats, too aesthetically emphasizes the need to cleanse the spiritual sickness of the modern man. Yeats feels himself devastated at the emergence of the new beastly and savage culture in which he finds himself alien. The emergence of savage culture devoid of the ethical, aesthetic and spiritual dimensions of life makes Yeats disillusioned. Yeats writes; 'a vast image out of spiritus Mundi Troubles my sight'. In 'Sailing to Byzantium', Yeats seeks emancipation by 'Studying moments of its own magnificence'. The real emancipation to Yeats lies in getting spiritually cleansed. In order to achieve spiritual perfection, Yeats calls upon the 'holy sages' of Byzantium to 'consume' his spiritual sickness. He calls upon the holy sages to be his 'Singing masters' and to gather him into the 'artifice of eternity'. In the realm of Yeasts' Poetry, emancipation has been sought and contemplated in terms of exercising the dictates of the soul on the body. The dichotomy of the matter and spirit is thus an indirect outcome of the lack of applicability of the ethical and aesthetic principles of love. Love in Maugham world bears a metaphysical and mystical connotations taking man to the Unknown. Philip-Mildred relationship opens up a new horizon for making the invisible aesthetic patterns of life visible. Woman, in the Shavian world, has been made a means of procreating a better generation for making the planet earth worth-living. Woman in Maugham's world is lacklustre, pale and anemic. Mildred's lacklustre and anemic physiognomy paradoxically possesses within a power of making Philip alienated to the mainstream of the conventional society. The more Mildred is indifferent to Philip's need of communicating to her the more he feels lonely and alienated to the dictates of the 'real' world. The plight of Larry is no different from that of Philip. Larry too in an identical way declines to conform to the cult of Americanism. Larry is lacerated at the bemoanings of the self. Julia too feels her 'self thwarted and threatened in the theatrical world while sitting at the periphery of the theatre. She obliquely looks at the 'real' images of men and women who come onto the stage and play their roles with pomp and show—bears an ironical meaning. To her it is not 'they' rather it is she who is the real artist in the true sense. It can thus dialectically be argued that the real meaning of creativity lies not in succumbing to the spiritually hollow real world. Maugham thus gives a new twist and turn; a new dimension of creativity in the post-modern society. Maugham as such points out at the new attitude of art, love, beauty and creativity. The real art, beauty, love and craftsmanship thus remain ensconced in man's putting up his stance of life in the image he has been created.

In Tagore's dynamics of freedom, it is the 'reason' on which the axis of freedom moves. In his poem, 'where the mind is without fear',—reason plays a vital role in making India a heaven of freedom. Getting involved in the parochial disputes, superstition and arrogance, says Tagore, would be tantamount to yielding to bondage. Tagore talks of complete fulfilment of the cherished dreams of freedom. Nissim Ezekiel who comes of the Indo-Anglian backgrounds, rationalistically argues to adhere to 'a cold lucidity' in order to protect Man from guilt and temptation of the mundane world. John Bunyan in his 'Pilgrim's progress' biblically projects man bent up carrying the burden of bondage in the mundane world. Emancipation would remain illusive to man, says Bunyan, if he stoops to the seven deadly sins. In his poem 'philosophy', Ezekiel biblically explores the metaphysical and the mystical wisdom elaborating that the invisible divine forces mysteriously remain operative in human life. Ezekiel ardently argues that spiritual regeneration remains operative in Man's not yielding to temptation and guilt. In Maugham's realm of fiction, yielding to passion embroils man into the tentacles of bondage. Ezekiel while exploring his 'enterprise' of life rationalistically looks at mundane life with 'a cold lucidity' restraining varied forms of bondage, guilt and temptation. From Ezekiel's rationalistic vision, it is the firm resolution of not yielding to temptation alone creates emancipation. Ezekiel biblically writes; 'Home is where we have to gather grace'. Maugham like Balzac is an objective observer of the prevailing intricacies of human life. Balzac had nothing in common with the realistic novelists. Even his French admirers realized elements of melodrama in his realistic writing. 'I have often been astonished', wrote Baudlaire, 'that the great glory of Balzac was to pass for an observer. It has always seemed to me that his principal merit was to be a visionary and a passionate visionary. In 'Com'edie humain' Balzac's characters move round money, lust and magic. As Balzac is a great realist, the problem of money has realistically been exposed in his 'Com'edie humain'. The society Balzac belonged was obsessed with money. Money is the basic driving force in many of his novels. The less money a man possesses the more violent he becomes. Balzac realistically argues that money is the chief motivator for making man hanker after lust, magic and money. The world Balzac presents is a world in which guilt; obsession and lust remain implicit to their being. Magic in Balzac's 'Com'edie humain', in reality is another means of attaining uninhibited thirst for power, money and lust. Balzac braces up the instrument of morality while making his characters bridled with the desire of power, magic, money and lust. Life without melodrama is inconceivable but Balzac realistically believes that the possession of wealth either acquired by trickery or by magic leads to doom and down fall. In Maugham's 'Magician', Hado is a devil incarnate. He conjures up black art to feed his cannibalistic desires. Margaret is made hypnotized to cater to his libido. Evil in Maugham's world lies deep-seated and camouflaged below the fair show. The 'fair' of the 'painted veil' in Maugham's depiction of evil has a paradoxical meaning. Strickland in Maugham's 'The moon and six pence' is obsessed with deriving pleasure on the physical plain. In Maugham's exploration of human predicament, 'Sexual instinct' plays a vital role in defining the motley colours of the self. The rebellion against the established order and the social milieu crops up surreptitiously in man. Getting awakened to a new reality Strickland forsakes his domesticity to see his invisible instinctual patterns of life visible in the 'far from the madding crowd'. Magic ensconced with lust can be realistically seen persisting in Maugham's 'Magician'. Hado casts magical spell to cater to his hedonistic pleasure. Margaret is magically hypnotized to make her yield to Hado's hedonism. In 'Of Human Bondage', and 'The Razor's Edge' man has been shown struggling against the power of money and the man-made altruistic means of emancipating society. Larry is lured into the business of the happiness principle—in which money with all its power of dehumanizing man casts a corrupting influence. Larry unlike Isabel acts what is contrary to the ethics of the American principle of happiness according to which money is taken to be the touchstone of success. Larry who is averse to the idea of living a life of the happiness-principle doesn't desire for taking happiness in both his hands. Philip frantically runs away from Blackstable to various places in order to aesthetically see how the squalor and poverty are themselves are greater reality. His experiences in both Heidelberg and Paris create in him an urge to look into the Unknown. Frau Daughters during his sojourn in Heidelberg aspire for coming up their mundane living. Fraulein Thelka can't marry the man she is already engaged to, as the young man's father is an Indian rubber merchant doesn't approve of their marriage. Fraulein Hedwig is another girl living in Professor Erlin's house. Her condition is no different from that of Thelka. She is daughter of merchant belonging to Berlin. Fraulein Anna is an idealist who believes in putting great stress upon character. She is foredoomed to live a life of spinsterhood. Man thus in Maugham's world feels his 'self threatened at the oddities of the situation he is pitted against. Eliot's usage of strange symbols, allusions and images associated with spiritual degeneration emphasize the new kind of rhetoric and vehicle of communicating the poetic verse. Lawrence employs images symbolizing the need to re-integrate society with a new vision of hope, reconciliation and spiritual joy. Eliot like Lawrence realistically perceives the decay of the 19th century conventional society. Maugham dialectically draws up a line of the demarcation between fact and fiction. Curtis Anthony while reviewing Maugham's art of fiction, writes; "Maugham believed in both magic and the effort better than anyone he knew that the path to the former was only through the later. As a writer he was with the sorcerer and the opportune". As Maugham was disillusioned with the realistic cult of writing he dialectically knew that the jargons of the scientific establishments hardly have propensity to accommodate the innate instincts that implicitly remain at work from within. George Orwell too in an identical way reposes his faith in the 'proles'. 'If there is hope, wrote Orwell, it lies in the proles'. Further Curtis Anthony ratiocinates how Maugham gave up the idea of writing in the manner of fin-de-siecle. In the beginning of his writings, Maugham had aspired for writing "In the ornate manner of the fin-de-siecle but in the first book he turned to style of writing which aimed to be naturalistic".

Both Somerset Maugham and D.H. Lawrence enthusiastically explore Man's relation with the self. The anguish to define the self in the alien surroundings provides Maugham's protagonists the fire and brimstones for the survival of the individual. Lawrence through his new form and technique of experimental novels in which man has been shown struggling against the constraints of sex and bondage points out at the emergence of the neo-mechanical and industrial backgrounds. Both Maugham and Lawrence in identical ways project man adjusting his self with the new emerging values emanating from the colossal growth of science and intellect. In 'Sons and lovers', Lawrence presents the duality of man in the new industrial world. Paul is caught up in a typical Oedipal situation. He is a split personality in the sense that he seeks spiritual consolation in Miriam and physical attachment in Clara. The nature of bond which Lawrence realistically explores is different from that of bondage shown in the domain of Maugham's novels. The new form of Lawrence's novel is traditional but experimental in nature on account of the emergence of the new mechanical society, which pushes man into throes of duality and dilemma. Lawrence thus brings into focus the new challenges emerging from the enormity of the industrialized society. In Rainbow he explores the new intricacies of the modern living that enmeshes man in all its unprecedented human conditions. The ever-growing humanism says Maugham, ironically brought a sea change to the complex condition of the modern society. The strange allusions taking place in the new industrial settings open up the new horizon in which man while passing through the colossal growth of the mechanical society, feels his 'self threatened. Both Maugham and Lawrence thus experience a real anguish for the reintegration of the self in the spiritually fragmented society. The urge to reintegrate and readjust the self with the new industrial and mechanical setup, finds expression in Maugham's novels. For Maugham reintegrating the 'self with the 'real' world, can be achieved by concentrating on the inertia of the self—is essential for achieving greater reality. Maugham's novels like 'The moon and six pence'; 'Cakes and Ale' and 'The painted veil' portray characters built up on the solipsistic technique. Lawrence on the other hand is closer to blood than to ink.

Maugham like Shaw is a rebel. Shaw through his dramatic personae ridicules the socialistic claims of making the earth a heaven of freedom. The sense and sensibility evoked in the Shavian world create an urge to retrieve man from economic deprivation. The socialistic philosophy propounded by Marx and Engels compartmentalized man into 'haves' and 'have-nots' giving a new meaning and connotation of loneliness. Shaw on the one hand makes emotions subdued to reason de tour, Maugham on the other hand while delineating his dialectical vision says that emotion of multitudes has a being of their own. The dark, savage and subliminal emotions implicit in the being of man get evocative and manifest in the behavioral patterns of human relationships. Maugham thus applies the dialectical approach to probe and see how man can free himself from the subliminal and dark savage passions. In Maugham's domain of dialectics, it is the linking up of the colossal growth of intellect with aesthetics that can truly project real emancipation. In a bid to escape from the spiritual degeneration of the modern world Yeats yarns for 'studying the monuments of its own magnificence'. Maugham aesthetically seeks greater realities in order to have a foothold, succor and sustenance in the modern world. Maugham like Lawrence builds up human relationship taking into accounts the new grounds and experiences that threaten human aspirations of living at par with the knowledge of the self. Lawrence projects his novels on the technique of depicting human relationships on the patterns of blood intimacy. Maugham on the other hand projects his novels on the solipsistic technique. Unlike G. B. Shaw, Graham Greene, Evelyn Waugh and George Orwell, Maugham explores deep, calm and smouldering emotions which ultimately get evocative seeking participation in the building up of human relationships. Behavioral relationships, says Maugham, apart from the realistic presentation of art and life are an indirect outcome of those invisible dark savage passions. Maugham's main business is to make the invisible dark passions visible on the dialectical plane. Eliot in his various critical essays emphasizes the intermingling of the past with the present. He opines that the 'existing' order needs to be re-adjusted with the past in order to take creative processes in the correct perspective. Eliot on the one hand, emphasizes the 'extinction of personality'; Maugham on the other hand dialectically argues that the dark savage passions and 'black despair' have a being of their own. His characters remain caught up into the web of aesthetic emotion. A dialectical approach to life and art thus says Maugham can take man to the road of freedom by aesthetically spiritualizing the ever-growing enormity of intellect at every existing order.

1
Portrait of the Artist

Maugham's dialectics of freedom explores various naunces of art and morality. The fictional art Maugham projects, forms a balance between his ethics and aesthetics. The exequisite beauty, art, clairvoyance and the flamboyant emotions which he intermingles with his dialectical art, create artistic elevation enabling man to come up the mundane realities he finds himself beset with. Maugham is basically a novelist of aesthetic sensibility. He is conscious of the factors which always remain at the back of the human mind which act getting transmuted into a palatable force logistically reasoning out the instinctual and behaviourial patterns of human relationships with a mystical insight. Maugham's love of literature and society, thus makes an indelible imprint into the human psyche. Maugham at the same time, never divulges from the assertion of morality in his presentation of his fictional art. It can thus rationalistically be argued that there is reciprocal and implied relation between the ethics and aesthetics he explores. It would be uneven to limit Somerset Maugham to be merely a Naturalistic Writer. To attribute him to be merely a Naturalistic Writer, would be tantamount to presenting an incomplete picture of the artist Maugham was. Shaw was a disillusioned romanticist provoking laughter at the prevailing shackles of the romantic sensibility. In his exposition of the realistic society, Shaw chose to play the role of a realist making the rationale to be the basis of probing of the intricacies of human problems. Maugham on the other hand was a disillusioned realist. Being conscious that realism was no more relevant to explore the ambiguities which the colossal growth of the science had dismantled man both spiritually and existentially. Maugham in the post modern era thus applies the dialectical art to fill up those ambiguities of the collocations of atoms with his aesthetic and ethical insight. Maugham with no less vigour emphasizes the elemental, primitive and instinctual forces which exist as subliminal undercurrents of the streams of human consciousness and determine the shape of things to come in various syllogistic propositions.

As Maugham is a complete artist with a dialectical vision, he has a mystical insight to see the limitations of science that embroil man into the annals of alienation and rootlessness. Maugham aesthetically probes the 'ambiguities' which are a by-product of the scientific facts which end up with the cessation of the spiritual values. The 'ambiguities' inculcated by the new scientific order, says Maugham, always remain at the back of the substance of the human mind pushing him into the endless labyrinth of loneliness and despair. But Maugham who is essentially an optimist, never loses hope in the renovation of the human spirit and explicates the mystery of the human existence from the dialectical perspective. The exponents of the Socialistic philosophy saw hope and renovation in dialectical materialism which ended up with disillusionment, despair and pessimisn. This enabled Maugham to say that man need not get bemused at the colossal growth of scientific, intellectual, industrial and above all dialectical materialism.

Maugham thus naturalises the scientific facts which found its culmination in the diminution of the ethical, mystical and metaphysical values. Maugham as such aesthetically spiritualises the colossal growth of the scientific facts. Unlike Freud, Maugham humanistically pinpoints those integrals of the self which project the whole identity of man. To Maugham, the doctrine of the inner self is a parapet through which man can evolve a dialectical mechanism to expose the illusiveness of the 'real' world with all its preponderance. Maugham was greatly influenced by Maupassant and Emile Zola whose ethics of Naturalism had made an indelible imprint on his life and works. Maugham is no less influenced by Spinoza who regards Man's enunciation of good and evil as self-illusory. Thus the doctrine of the innerself, to Maugham, is the yardstick through which he defines the self in the alien surroundings. Maugham doesn't get bewildered at the ever growing and evolutionary processes that bring about change in the human perception and existentially dismantle man in his search of knowing the riddle of the human existence. Instead, the basic instincts, mysteriously work within and act as a palatable force in every assertion of human behaviour. Frome who belongs to the post-Freudian era, too, like Maugham. Psychoanalitically agrues that the psycho-analytical study, alone doesn't constitute the whole being of man. Instead the instinct implicit in the being of man, too plays a crucial role in adding up and enhancing the evergrowing human consciousness. It is in this sense that Maugham finds the conventional ethics dysfunctional and inoperative. As such he stresses the need to open up 'the third dimension' bringing into focus those emotions of multitude and the impulses which are themselves a larger reality. The ethics of Naturalism, to Somerset Maugham, is not an end but a means to make the abstract morality operative. The 'real' world existing on the mere physical plane, says Maugham is self-illusory. Maugham hence applies the dialectical art to project a larger reality to bring about a total transformation to the spiritually sterile society. Realism which is found to be inadequate in Maugham's dialectics of freedom, ironically takes into account the experiences merely existing at the physical plane. Maugham therefore employs the dialectical method to streamline and bring into harmony both the scientific and instinctive patterns of life. Maugham saw that the real emancipation lay in rather spiritualising the 'senses'. What is striking is that Maugham concentrates on the inertia of the self which to him becomes the scaffolding for communicating to the real world. Like Bergson, Maugham too believes that it is the ever growing consciousness which depicts the shape of things to come; the human psyche is made to be remoulded and re-shaped with every flux of the human consciousness for a better co-ordination and communication between the self and the 'real' world. In Maugham's convas of the dialectial art the inertia of the self enables him to put up his stance of life.

As Eliot was influenced by the Indian mythology, Maugham was no less influenced by the ethics of mysticism practised by the Indian saga of mystics. To him, achieving the path of salvation is something akin to walking tip toe on to the 'Razor's Edge'; this is how Maugham's mysticism and vision lie ensconced into the wisdom of the Indian philosophy. George Orwell saw hope of redemption in striking a balance between the 'Yogi and the Commissar'. In 'The Moon and six pence' Maugham paints the stoic, sublime and primitive landscapes showing how he was greatly influenced by the writers like Kalidasa and Epicetus. In 'The Moon and six pence' Maugham like Kalidasa and Epicetus unfolds the stoic landscapes of asceticism and renunciation of life. The self-realization in Kalidasa can be seen in the forlorn and stoic landscapes. In 'Of human Bondage', the metaphysics of love is realised in denying the pursuit of happiness. Like D.H.Lawrence, Maugham revels in yielding to the primitive, elemental, dark and savage passions which 'in full throated ease' hold man in a state of bondage.

As Maugham is an existentialist, he draws up a line between essence and existence. The conventional ethics as Maugham saw was spiritually lack-lustre. The 'new' man as such, says Maugham dialectically looks up for a way out to come out from the conventional ethics which no more caters to his aesthetic and metaphysical aspirations of life. Maugham is an optimist believing in the gospel of the apocalypse. He makes assertion of his stance of life saying that man in the post modern era in which he has been made servile to the mechanical society, needn't be bemused; instead, he optimistically delineates the concept of freedom which to him alone can take him to self-fulfilment and emancipation. Marx and Engels, on the other hand saw redemption in dialectical materialism. Maugham on the other hand, says that man is not the product of the being; rather he is what is experiences to be. There could be real attainment of freedom and self-fulfilment if man applies the dialectical approach to life. In 'The Summing up' he shows his adherence to morality. As

Maugham regards good and evil self illusory, he practically applies the implied objectivity in his understanding of man and his environs. In fact, by applying his dialectical art Maugham intends to make man come up the illusiveness of the 'real' world. A dialectical approach to the human existence, thus says Maugham, alone can retrieve man from human bondage.

2
Ethics and Aesthetics

With the beginning of human civilization, the search for freedom has been the basic impetus to know the intricacies of human life with all its exquisite charms and piquant colours. The incessant human endeavour to delve deep into the unknowableness of the innate being receives impetus from the basic driving force of unentwining man from centuries long suffering creating a propensity to unfold self expression and individual freedom from their belief; 'know thy self'. In the fifth century B. C. the Hellenic philosopher of Abdera. Opined that "Man is the measure of all things"[1]. The Hellenic saw in Man "the lord of creation"[2]. Arnold Toynbee tracing the generic attributes of the Hellenic civilization, writes that "The Hellenic gods were accessible to man because they had been created by man, in man's image; the God of Israil was accessible to Man because he had created man in his own image[3]. Toynbee takes note of the self-assertion which was deeply embedded to the fabric of the Hellenic civilization had the reflection of its spirits even after Christianity manifested itself as a revealed religion.The emergence of Christianity says Toynbee had made the Hellenic civilization dysfunctional but essence of the Hellenic spirit made itself manifest in the spectre of Christianity. Toynbee writes; "In Hellenic philosophy

Christianity found an intellectual medium for the statement of Christian beliefs in terms acceptable to an Hellenically educated minority of society"[4]. Human nature has always been discerned as an enigma; a conundrum to the world at large. William Shakespeare who exhibits sympathetic insight. While depicting the conundrum of human nature, finds himself awestruck at the human attributes, 'What a piece of work is a man!' this is how Shakespeare shows his love for the mankind. Jonathan swift who envisions human nature with a tinge of cynicism, and contempt points out at man's depravity. Philip Lee Ralph goes through the history of human civilization at length probes human nature with an objective insight and writes, "Man has been described as but little lower than the angels, as a vile worm, as a free agent, as a helpless puppet, as good, bad, and as a mixture of all these"[5]. But great is Man's impetuosity of the incessant quest for emancipation to unburden himself from the onslaught of 'human bondage'. Philip Lee Ralph at length throws light over the Hellenic civilization and points out at their perspicacity to define their "Positive contribution"[6]. Leading man to the evocativeness of "Christianity through the injection into Judaism of the counter Jevish idea of incarnation"[7]. Keeping in view the rise and fall of civilization in the historical perspective, Toynbee co-relates their roots and inter-connection of civilizations; "The prophets were children of another civilization in disintegration; Christianity was born of the sufferings of a disintegrating Graeco-Roman world"[8]. Commenting on the generic attributes of defining their 'self' which lay deeply embedded to the Hellenic civilization. Philip Lee Ralph like Toynbee points out at their instinctual patterns of life which went on to permeate into the psyche of the successive generation; "The primitiveness of their religion proved a stumbling block to the Greeks even when they shook of creed and fable sought to define the good in purely humanistic terms"[9]. Even Socrates went to say that "unexamined life is not worth-living"[10]. The Hellense, hence, ardently believed that 'Man is the measure of all things'[11]. John Bunyan in the sixth century B.C. emphasizes the need to live a life of spiritual elevation which he regards as, 'Pilgrim's Progress'. Marx and Engels had a different approach to life. They laid emphasis on the Socialistic revolution for they saw attainment of freedom in 'dialectical materialism'[12]. Freedom meant to them a mere attainment of economic prosperity for bridging up the gap between the 'haves' and 'havenots'. The dream of retrieval from the drudgery of the feudal system as foreseen in the socialistic revolution gave vent to dialectical materialism. The Wellsyan Utopia argued for inculcation of the scientific order which ironically ended up in the 'Brave New World'. Somerset Maugham who drew inspiration from Flaubert's aesthetic sensibility apocalyptically looked for, a way of life for defining the self, in a society which found its culmination in the materialistic evolution of society. As such understanding man and his relationship in a world in which everything is connotated in terms of the aesthetic sensibility, is the basic driving force behind Maugham's artistic, literary and dialectical approach to life.

What needs to be emphasized is that Maugham by his dialectical art basically probes whether the scientific and technological developments has elaborated a complete understanding of Man and the Modern World, Maugham quizzically looks to the world he lives in and existentially probes human existence and its relation with the universe. Shakespeare in his plays agonizingly gets perturbed at the inexplicable labyrinth of human suffering. Thomas Hardy was conscious of the invisible forces which he says, remain at work mysteriously in human life. In Hardy's tragic world, the dark, baser, elemental and fatalistic forces frustrate the human endeavour of entering the promised land of freedom. Man inescapably finds himself caught up by the dark, mysterious and invisible forces of destiny. Hardy concentrates on the invisible in his exploration of manifold human suffering. As the 'invisible' remains unperceivable to man, he is deprived of all the joy of life he dreams of. Unlike Hardy and Oscar Wilde, Maugham finds mystery in the 'visible' which makes man entwined into the semblance of beauty. Oscar Wilde on the other hand aesthetically writes; "The true mystery of the world is the visible, not the invisible"[13]. Daniel Defoe in his master-piece novel, 'Robinson crusoe' projects Man pathetically struggling against the odds of the elemental forces, thrown upon him. Maugham applies the dynamics of Dialecticism and opines that the spice of human life lies implicit in the incessant human endeavour. Maugham looks beyond the mechanics of the scientific order and intends to know the unknowableness of human relationships taking into account not only the doctrine of the innerself but also of the varied collocations of science which remain instrumental in making the mettle of the modern world. Maugham hence dialectically explores those areas of 'darkness'. Which holds the soul in a state of human bondage. Being a keen observer of human life Maugham practises complete objectivity and detachment while exploring various naunces of human relationships for a better co-ordination between ethics and aesthetics. Maugham's dialectical art thus projects an objective vision to explore the 'heart of the matter' in consonance with the inculcation of the Neo-mechanical order. In his remarkable essay, "In variation on a theme", Maugham intends to explore human life with all its iota of shades and designs. Maugham unlike the Pre-Raphaelites and the Romantics inescapably takes up life as it emerges to him. Maugham writes; "I am not a critic and it is not my business to criticise."[14]. In 'The writer's point of view', Maugham adopts a more realistic approach to life and goes on to say that innate feelings and instinctual patterns of life play a pivotal role in making the being of Man. Maugham writes; "What-ever he writes is the expression of his personality and it is the manifestation of his innate feelings, his experience and his opinions"[15], doesn't mean that he divulges from the moral and spiritual dimensions of human life and the instinctual patterns which play a pivotal role in making the being of Man. Maugham writes; "What ever he writes is the expression of his personality and it is the manifestation of his innate feelings, his experience and his opinions"[16], does't mean that he divulges from the moral and spiritual dimensions of human life. Oscar Wilde in an identical way too interprets human life in terms of the aesthetic aspects and opines that "I never approve, or disapprove, of anything now. It is an absurd attitude to take towards life. We are not sent into the world to air our moral prejudices. I never take any notice of what common people say, and I never interfere with what charming people do. If a personality fascinates me, whatever mode of expression that personality selects is absolutely delightful to me"[17].

Maugham is thus basically a novelist of aesthetic sensibility. The aesthetic sensibility projected on the convas of his fictional art, is not an end but a means of making assertion of the moral and spiritual strength. His assertion that the "aim of writer of fiction I repeat is not to instruct but to please"[18]. Maugham's exploration of passion, art and beauty is part of his literary, artistic, aesthetic and above all dialectical approach to life, is to establish harmonious relation between art and morality; truth and beauty. Such realistic presentation of human life, from Maugham's dialectical perspective, builds up and projects the concept of the 'beautiful'[19], to 'please'[20] sense and sensibility. The problem of loneliness emanating from the collocations of the scientific facts makes Maugham essentially conscious of the basic reasons causing schism between flesh and spirit; body and soul. His anguish to define the self in a strange world in which the conventional morality remains indifferent to the aesthetic, mystical and metaphysical aspects of human life flares up loneliness and despair. Such dissipation and dismantling of the human and spiritual values make Maugham essentially a rebel. Hence Maugham's ethics and aesthetics remain entwined with each other for a saner and fuller realization of ethical and aesthetic realizations of human life. Maugham writes; "Fiction is an art and the purpose of art is to please. I can only suppose it is because of the unfortunate impression. So wildly held that there is something shameful in pleasure. But all pleasure is good. Only some pleasure is mischievous consequences and it is better to eschew them"[21]. It thus shows how the element of morality lies deep-seated into the texture of his novels. Maugham was essentially influenced by the classical masters. Plato logically argues that all poets should be banished from the ideal republic. But the imperative meaning implicit in it points out at dismantling licentiousness and immorality. Maugham thus finds solace in catering to the needs of the 'soul'. What needs to be emphasized that he takes stock of the modern human condition in order to probe the basic reasons causing anguish, loneliness and alienation in the modern context. From Maugham's dialectical perspective, loneliness is a by-product of Man's inability to live a viable life of his 'self'. His aesthetic sensibility makes inroads into the human psyche and helps us understand the multifoliate and complex being of Man in respect of the world and the universe as a whole. The anguish to re-orient and re-organise the 'self' in the strange and spiritually alienated world, gives him the basic impetus to evolve the dialectical doctrine in order to present how aesthetic beauty makes indelible imprint on the inner recesses of the human psyche. In Somerset Maugham's pneumatology, aesthetic art is the 'life force' which infuses the idea of the beautiful into the human consciousness and aesthetically inspires man for a harmonious living. Man says Somerset Maugham listens to every throb of the heart. Like D. H. Lawrence, Aldous Huxley and Arnold Bennet, Maugham shares the anguish of the contemporaenous society. As he belongs to the tradition of Flaubert, Baudlair, Emile zola and Maupassant, he feels the lack-lustre life of the conventional morality in which man ironically remains stranger in the modern world. Unlike Sydney Maugham doesn't give a scornful look to laughter and holds 'pleasure' something akin to 'moving transport of poetry'[22]. Maugham's idea of the 'beautiful' is no less significant than Graham Greene's emphasis on 'catholicity'. Such dialectical perspective makes his heart leap with joy as he aesthetically beholds the elemental machination of the stark savage passions. These basic instincts compel him to define the motley colours of the self. In George Orwell's exploration of the human psyche, feelings are put up in the garb of the 'double speake'. On the other hand, Maugham's protagonists remain true to the manifold dimensions of the self. Any violation of the ethics of the soul is tantamount to dismantling the identity and human existence.

Maugham aesthetically looks to the reason of Man's spiritual loneliness as such Maugham stresses the need to take into account the inborn, psychic and instinctual patterns of human behaviour which play a pivotal role in creating a harmonious living in the society man lives in. Such palpable and subtle emotions make empathy and provide insight for building up of human relationship. Having taken into account this basic driving force which plays a pivotal role in shaping up the human psyche, Maugham says that alienation from the mainstream of life, gets cropped up on account of Man's in- ability to find a communion between the 'self' and the outside world. What needs to be emphasized is that Maugham introspects and probes the factors giving rise to spiritual imbecility, rootlessness and alienation from the mainstream of life.The basic identity which lay at the back of the mind becomes evocative in the externalites of human behaviour. What is bewildering to Maugham's protagonists is the sudden awareness of the 'self' through which they build up their identity and make a harmonious relation between the self and the real world: Maugham's protagonists remain true to the motley dimensions of the 'self'.

Maugham is critical of the conventional morality in which the principle of beauty is kept off the mainstream of life. Maugham's concept of the 'beautiful' is thus a vehicle which moves up and ennobles man to act in a virtuous manner making man feel every throb of the self on the aesthetic, mystical and instinctual planes. Maugham in his various writings—novels, short stories, plays and even in his critical essays, point out at the ennobling power of the aesthetic experience. 'Pleasure in Maugham's dynamics of dialecticism, has a constructive role of ennobling power for building up a spiritually elevated society wherein man lives in complete harmony with the 'self' and the outside world. William Wordsworth in an identical way perceives how beauty takes man from the mundane to the transcendental plane. Beauty says Wordsworth has a two fold function—perception and transcendence; 'My heart leaps up when I behold', is suggestive of how the idea of the 'beautiful' plays a concilatory role and bridges up man and his environs. The 'Instinctive distaste' implict in Mildred makes Philip undergo self-inflictment and loneliness. Maugham writes: "there must have been some strange morbidity in his nature which made him take a grim peasure in self torture"[23].

Somerset Maugham's perspicacity and clairvoyance to define passion in all its manifold colour and shades, are part of his dilectical perspective which in turn enables him to create characters in his own image. Maugham thus is conscious of the urge to explore whatever is hidden and deep-seated in him. Maugham solipsistically writes; "It may be asked why, if I turned Paul Gauguin into an English man, I could not do the same with the persons of this book. The answer is simple: I couldn't. They wouldn't have been the people they are. I do not pretend that they are American as Americans see themselves; they are American seen through an English eye"[24]. Hence the artistic endeavour employed to make the subjective go futile while transmuting various ingredients of art into the organic whole. The inertia of the 'self' thus gets externalised and mixed up with the visage of the behavioural patterns of society. Maugham writes; "Whatever he writes is the expression of his personality and it is the manifestation of his innate instincts, his feelings, and his opinions. How ever hard he tries to be objective he remains the slave of his ideosyncracies. However hard he tries to be impartial he can't help taking sides"[25]. Showing disagreement with T.S. Eliot's concept of objectivity, Maugham realistically perceives possibility of shreds of subjectivity in every work of art. In his remarkable novels, 'Of human bondage' and 'The Razor's Edge', Maugham explores the fury of passions which hold human soul in a state of bondage and shows how man who is a strange piece of work, is vulnerable to the fury of passions and dark elemental forces of nature. Man, says Somerset Maugham, goes on to remain entrapped and caught up into the web of the savage passions. Maugham on the one hand asserts that "I am not a critic and it is not my business to please"[26]. Philip Sydney on the other hand opines that the function of a poet is "to instruct"[27]. Unlike Maugham's emphasis on 'Pleasure', creative imagination and instruction go hand in hand in Sydney's definition of creative art. Hence from Maugham's aesthetic standpoint 'pleasure' is the basic driving force from which emanates various iota of passion and instincts which remain instrumental in the making of the self. As Maugham is pre-occupied with the inertia and emotion of multitude, he knows no escape from those flamboyant emotions and basic instincts which work as under currents enhancing the human consciousness for a better framework of communicating with the real world. It is this context in which Maugham elaborates the collective psyche and the way the identity of man needs to be interpreted and analyzed in the modern world. Unlike Maugham, Lawrence interprets the basic identity of Man in terms of the blood-intimacy. Maugham eloquently writes; "For all the characters that we create are but copies of the ourselves. It is that they really are nobler, more disinterested and virtuous and spiritual than I it is very natural that they being god-like they should create men in their own image".[28] By inculcating the technique of solipsisim Maugham concentrates on the inertia of the self which in turn gets manifest in the externalities of human behaviour. Being conscious of the inertia that solipsistically plays a pivotal role in the unfolding of the 'self' in the face of the world at large. Maugham emphatically asserts the need to grow up novels of the naturalistic trends. By intermingling the ethics and aesthetics, he makes inroads into the human psyche and builds up the canvas of his dialectical art. P. G. Wodehouse unlike Maugham points out at two ways of writing novels. Wodehouse writes; "I believe there are two ways of writing novels. One is mine, making a sort of musical comedy without music and ignoring real life altogether; the other is going right deep down into life and not carving a damn"[29]. Unlike P. G. Wodehouse, Maugham applies the Naturalistic flair of writing to search for greater realities of life. Maugham thus belongs to the post modern era in order to emphasize the 'third dimension of the unexplored self. Maugham on the other hand while defining the art of fiction, emphasizes the enjoyableness of "reading a good novel", and dialectically writes; "And I should like to remind you that reading should be enjoyable"[30]. Walter Allen in an identical way establishes a co-relationship between the characters an auther creates and the values inherent therein. Walter Allen commenting 'on the art of Novel' writes; "This is why in judging a novel we are faced with the task of assessing not only the author's ability to create characters, for instance, but also the values inherent in the characters and their behaviour".[31] Unlike T.S. Eliot, Maugham while functioning as a critic, identifies new frontiers of criticism. Walter Allen on the other hand and says that the "novelist is free to choose his material only in a limited sense, and his choice is governed by the deepest compulsions of his personality. It is these that dictate both the nature of his novels and the conclusions about life he expresses through them"[32].

Maugham in his Dialectics of freedom utilises his literary and fictional effort to synchronise the primitive and instinctual patterns of life in a dialectical whole. Maugham's characters never lookback instead they remain prisoner of the 'self. Their scrambling to difine their 'self' doesn't however axphysiate their urge to unfetter themselves from the inclemence of human bondage. "A novel, as such says Walter Allen, is a totality, made up of all the words in it, and it must be judged as a totality. Of this totality characterisation is only a part ...."[33].

Somerset Maugham's fictional art is thus based on the solipsistic and the aesthetic art. The aesthetic art in Maugham's opinion in the true sense is the 'interpreter of all maladies'. Like Virginia Woolf, Flaubert, James Joyce and D. H. Lawrance, Maugham concentrates on the inward experience. Awareness of the self is an act of introspection which is meant to play a meaningful role in infusing anguish and agony within the human psyche in order to come up the human predicament. What needs to be explored is that Maugham's is protagonists remain embued with zest and get frenzied in order to live up to the aspirations of the soul. Man in Maugham's exploration of aesthetic beauty, never divulges from the innate human propositions giving impetus to define itself in every act of assertion in the mundane society. It is the doctrine of solipsism says Maugham which makes human relationship define its stance of life. Bertrand Russele in an identical way writes; "It is difficult to give a logically tenable account of this position without recognising that good and evil are subjective"[34]. Human relationships thus from the solipsistic standpoint, break, alter grow and even get metamorphosed in strange human conditions. In Maugham's dialectics of freedom, thus the aesthetic and instinctual aspects remain intermingled with the moral and spiritual spheres of life. The impulse in him gives impetus to get man unfettered from human bondage. Human bondage to passion, lust, temptation, gullibility and man's proneness to live a life of materialism, becomes a real obstacle to the attainment of transcedence evoking a sense of liberation. Maugham eloquently writes: "These conceptions not only appealed to my dramatic instinct, they filled me beside with a very delectable sense of liberation".[35] The aesthetic and spiritual dimensions implicit in man, open up a new vista of human propositions for his retrieval from the labyrinth of human bondage. Hence the connotation of loneliness in Maugham's realm of fiction, bears a different dimension from that of loneliness and spiritual embecility dealt within the parameter of Eliot's poetry.

The schism between ethics and aesthetics, says Somerset Maugham, is the root cause of Man's alienation and spiritual crises. From the dialectical standpoint, it is the real interpreter of all maladies in the modern context. In Eliot's poetry, Man has been shown perturbed at finding himself amputated and cut off from the mainstreem of tradition. Man with all his colossal attainment of knowledge, as Eliot depicts, ironically does'nt know how to address his problem of loneliness and his search for identity in the mechanistic society. Maugham looks more at ease in knowing the labyrinth of human suffering than judging it while delving deep into the paradox of human existence. Thus the impulse hidden beneath the serene surface of the external behaviour is the principal driving force which plays a pivotal role in the evocation of the self.

Such emotion of multitude and anxiety to define the self enables man to devise ways and means to present an objective pricture of human life by making his characters pitted against hostile and oblique situations. Bergson's elaboration of 'Elanvital' and D.H. Lawrance's, philosophy of blood intimacy—derive inspiration from the machanics of the art of subjectivity. Unlike Eliot, Maugham opines that all the artistic endeavour to make the subjective objective gets annihilated; "However hard to be objective he remains slave of his idiosyncracies. However hard he tries to be impartial he can't help taking sides[36]. It can thus dialectically be argued that assertion of morality lies deep-seated in Maugham's fabric of fictional art. The contours and concepts of freedom in Maugham's fictional and artistic realm, lie co-existed in getting emancipated from the whiff of passion ensnaring him into the knots of human bondage.

The modus operandi inculcated into the texture of Maugham's dialectics of freedom is upto a great extent different from that of Gautier, Baudlair, Flaubert and Oscar Wilde. As aestheticism ascribes art to be of paramount importance. Oscer Wilde another exponent of the school of Aestheticism evinces that the artistic and aesthetic beauty remain manifest in the principle of beauty. Wilde unwaveringly asserts that supermacy of art seeks perfection not from without but form within. Maugham's emphasis on the Naturalistic flair of writing is not an end but a means to probe Man's proclivity to 'happiness'. Oscar Wilde while probing the being of Man finds him either yielding to 'happiness' or to 'pleasure'. Dorian Gray introspects himself at length and comes to realize that "I have never searched for happiness, who wants happiness? I have searched for pleasure"[37]. Thus Man's indifference to the aesthetic beauty makes him devoid of the efficacy to feel the throbbing pulse of the self. From the existential point of view, man's inability to find a communion between ethics and aesthetics, gives rise to alienation from the mainstream of life. It can thus syllogistically be agrued that the Naturalistic technique inculcated in Maugham's dialectical art intends to probe the modern human condition. T. S. Eliot's in his poem, "The Wasteland" exposes the spiritual sterility of the modern age taking into account the colossal growth of the scientific facts. Maugham on the other hand laments at man's inability to perceive the 'beautiful'. Like Aldous Huxley, Somerset Maugham is at pains to say that all the paraphernalia of human progress inculcated in terms of the scientific, evolutionary and technological developments sought by man end up in the projection of the 'Brave New World'; all human aspirations of coming out of 'bondage', ironically end up in the dissipation of the self. W. B. Yeats, too belongs to the school of Aestheticism, laments at growing alienation, rootlessness and the spliting up of personality. Yeats also like Maugham finds man indifferent to the aesthetic, artistic and aristocratic values. Yeart symbolically writes;

The falcon cannot hear the falconer;
Things fall apart; the centre cannot hold;
Mere anarchy is loosed upon the world,
The blood-dimmed tide is loosed, and everywhere
The ceremony of innocence is drowned;[38]

The homelessness of the modern generation as depicted in Eliot's poetry, says Maugham, is thus a direct outcome of Man's pronenness to living a hedonistic life. Asto Man feels himself agonisingly perturbed at the colosal— Spiritual disintegration of his being—is the context in which both Eliot and Maugham in their identical ways explore Man's drying up of spiritual and human values. In this regard Eliot's 'The Wasteland" can be seen as a projection of a window dressing through which man's spiritually chaotic life has realistically been brought into focus. What makes Maugham bewildered is that he found both science and religion irreconcilable to each other. Keeping in view of the conflict operating between science and religion, Maugham applies the dialectical art in order to make science and religion in complete harmony. Maugham's dialectical endeavour thus emphasizes the need to open up a third dimension to re-adjust the human values in the new mechanistic society.

The writers like Andre'gid, Neitzche, Schopenhauer, Camus and Kirkegaard explicate the mystery of human life from the existential prospective.

Satre unlike Maugham draws nihilistic contours and ironically fails to notice pattern, music and design in the human existence. Satre writes, "It is certain that modern music is shattering forms, breaking away from conventions, carving it's own road. But exactly to whom does it speak of liberation, freedom, will of the creation of man by Man to a stale genteel listener whose ears are blocked by an idealist aesthetics"[39]. Disagreeing with Satre, Maugham believes in the apocalyptical philosophy and sees meaning, pattern, design and symphony in the human existence. As such he emphasizes the need to cultivate apocalyptical vision to see pattern and music in the human existence. As Maugham probes human existence from the existential stand point, he utilises his fictional effort to strike a balance between 'essence' and 'existence'. Man's indifference to aesthetic beauty, says Maugham, makes him devoid of the capability to realise the spiritual manifestation. From the existential stand point, lack of conformity between what man experiences himself to be and the colossal growth of the scientific facts, creates anguish and stifles his self. It can thus syllogistically be argued that the naturalistic trends inculcated in Maugham's art of fiction, is not an end but a means to probe the innate, behavioural patterns of the modern human condition. T. S. Eliot's 'The Wasteland', on the other hand explores the spiritual sterelity of the modern age taking into account the alienation and spiritual embecility; the corroding of the human values caused by the colossal growth of 'knowledge'[40]. Maugham on the other hand laments at main's inability to perceive the idea of the 'beautiful' and the naunces of aesthetics. Lord Tennyson who was the representative poet of the Victorian age, explores the conflict between science and religion. Tennyson in his representative poem, 'In Memorium', shows his preoccupation of the Victorian dilemma that had shaken up his belief. Perturbed at the conflict operating between science and relegion, Man has been shown bemused at the colossal growth of science. In order to come out of the Victorian dilemma, Tennyson tries to grip the tether of faith in the divine and the apocalyptical order. Knowledge, says Tennyson devoid of faith, is of no avail and vice versa. Maugham like Tennyson feels himself badly shaken up by the conflict operating between science and religion. Maugham like Robert Browning is wrapped up in the 'Robust' energy. He applies the mechanics of the dialectical art and makes both science and religion play a re-conciliatory role. Maugham who was influenced by Spinoza finds himself perturbed at the conflict operating between science and religion The basic problem that perturbed Maugham was how to make science religion and religion science. Freedom to Maugham meant for bracing up both science and religion in complete harmony. Commenting on Spinoza's concept of freedom, Lindsay writes; "This bringing together of science and religion in a form which was to be faithful to both was Spinoza's problem and what a problem it was. We shall understand better if we consider for a little how revolutionary and far reaching the implications of the new sciences were"[41]. With the emergence of the new scientific revolutions both Maugham and Spinoza, in identical ways found answers to the intricacies of human existence, in order to make science and religion cohere in complete agreement. Lindsay writes; "Both his science and his religion were to be uncompromising and in their uncompromising form they were to be brought together"[42]. Both good and evil says Spinoza are part of the illusory self. As such the inculcation of the mechanistic society gives man the semblance of illusion. It is in this sense that Maugham doesn't agree to the conventional ethics. As Maugham is essentially a rebel, he is always at logger-heads to give space to the anguish of his soul in a society which is indifferent to the ethical and aesthetic values. Nirad C. Chaudhuri, identifies this vacuum and stresses the need of "meeting the third dimension"[43] in order to unfold the embers of the fervid soul; "People from the tropics need a certain level of warmth inside and outside themselves to awaken their sense of actuality"[44]. The ethics propounded by Spinoza depends upon the attainment of knowledge. The human endeavour of linking up the finite with the infinite, says Spinoza, is the intellectual pursuit of knowledge. Both Spinoza and Kant commonly share the belief that the humanistic urges for aquisition of wisdom of the heart have the tenacity to transcend the limitation of the pursuit of knowledge.

Like Aldous Huxley, Somerset Maugham is at pains to say that all human progress ends up in the projection of the brave new world; all human aspirations for retrieving Man from the life of bondage, get reduced to the dissipation of the 'self'. Maugham explores the embers of anguish and ennui which suffocatingly thwart the being of man from within. Hence emotion of multitude remains instrumental in getting over the limitation of ratiocination. Spinoza thus in his exploration of ethics, braces up both the finite and the infinite substance by applying the theory of infinite modes. What man needs to attain is the intellectual and rationalistic persuit of life. Says Maugham, in order to put up the 'heart' on to the mantle of the infinite. All the mechanical and the rationalistic pursuit of life is thus not an end but a means to take man to the wholesomeness of the body and soul. The sum total of the finite in Maugham's dialectical vision thus construes to the infinite and the vice versa. The experience and 'knowledge' says Maugham donot necessarily bear negative connotations in his explication of the human existence. As such Man says Maugham is not needed to be bemused at the colossal growth of rationalization in the modern world. It dialectically explains how the spirit of rationalization and scientific temper too can explicate the spiritual, mystical and metaphiysical realizations of life. Edmund Spenser in his poem, 'Faerie Queene' takes ignorance to be bliss whereas Eliot takes the attainment of knowledge to be an obstacle to the aquisence of the spiritual and metaphysical aspects of human life. Eliot writes:

> "What is that sound high in the air
> Murmur of maternal lamentation
> Who are those hooded hordes swarming
> Over endless plains, stumbling in cracked earth[45].

In 'Ash Wednesday', Eliot projects the theme of resignation and surrender. The protagonist no more aspires for turning to the intellectual and materialistic persuit of life. Eliot writes :

> Because I do not hope to know again
> The infirm glory of the positive hour
> Because I do not think
> Because I know I shall not know
> The one veritable transitory power[46].

The writers like Neitzche, Schopenhauer, Albert Camus and Andre'gid, explicate the conundrum of life from the existential aspects whereas schopenhauer explores the melancholic nature of man. Henry James while elaborating the theory of art takes experience to be a condition to achieve transcendence. In 'portrait of a lady', Elizabeth intends to marry only when she would see the whole of Europe. A novelist says Henry James, gives shape to his life-like experiences and the language he employs acts as a vehicle through which he incarnates his characters in flesh and blood. He puts emphasis not merely on the independence of the novelist but also on the representation of the real life. Being conscious of the inner impulse, Maugham unlike Henry James adopts the naturalistic flare of writing and never affords to ignore the instinctual, primitive and elemental forces which mysteriously remain at work. Maugham thus feels the throbbing self which plays a significant role in the building up of Man's identity in the real world.

Mathew Arnold is too conscious of the 'bondage' that leads to 'anarchy' and dischord in human life.In 'culture and Anarchy' Arnold establishes the relation of the critic to the society. Being conscious of the elements of modernity, Arnold ardently argues that Man's proneness to "the pride, the sloth, the anger, the selfishness"[47], in the true sense, impairs the 'moral'[48] activity of man. Mathew Arnold in an identical way emphasizes intellectual deliverance which to him creates transcendence. Anrold however puts up two conditions for evolving his concept of freedom. As such Arnold's concept of "deliverance"[49], embodies the intermingling of the 'moral'[50] and intellectual "deliverance"[51]. Arnold writes; "But there is another deliverance for the human race, hardly less important, indeed, than the first—for in the enjoyment of both united consists man's true freedom—but demanded far less universally, and even more rarely and imperfectly hardly obtained; a deliverance neglected, apparently conceived, in some ages, while it has been pursued with earnestness in others, which derive from that very pursuit their peculiar character. This deliverance is an intellectual deliverance"[52]. Arnold projects his art and literature to assess how the elements of modernity causes moral hierarchy and dissipation of the moral and spiritual values. In his remarkable, essay "Culture and Anarchy" Arnold speaks of the inherent dangers of the disintegration of the human values. Arnold who upholds the canons of classicism is conscious of the prevalence of moral hierarchy which in his opinion, gives rise to 'Human bondage'. In Arnold's exploration of 'human bondage' it is the dismantling of the moral and intellectual aspects of life, which causes cultural anarchy. Arnold laments at the lack of 'sanity' that crops up directionlessness in the modern society. It is the lack of form, morality and 'sanity', says Arnold which causes choas and anarchy in the modern civilization. Arnold writes; "Sanity— that is the great virtue of the ancient literature: the want of that is the great defect of the modern, in spite of its variety and power"[53] Somerset Maugham explores human bondage in terms of man's getting entwined into 'passion'. Freedom says Mathew Arnold will remain incomplete unless 'intellectual deliverance' is achieved. To Arnold both the moral 'deliverance' and 'intellectual deliverance' are complementry to each other. 'Intellectual deliverance' is the key word which makes society embued with the modern spirit[54]. Maugham attributes his search of freedom to the deliverance which "consists in man's comprehension of the present and past".[55] A. Clutton–Brock Contemplating the naunces of art and aesthetic experience, elaborates the diverse experiences that shape up and enkindle the emancipating power of art. Brock writes; "If a work of art is good to me, its goodness is not moral but simply aesthetic, something perceived immediately and valued for its own sake, without relation to any kind of conduct"[56]. The emancipating power says A. Clutton—Brock lies not in the moral instead it lies in the aesthetic art. The aesthetic art defines A. Clutton—Brock is the state which "frees us from the chain of events which in other experiences bind us to our past and future"[57]. Speaking at length on the nature and art of experience Clutton emphasizes the transcedental quality of art which emancipates man from the life of fret and fever Clutton further writes; "The state of being aesthetic experience is not an abstract state; it uses all the content of other experience for its own purpose of freedom"[58]. J. A. Symonds in his essay 'Personal style' emphasizes the inborn and acquired faculties of human potentialities. Symonds traces inborn human attributes which play a crucial role in shaping up the genesis of Man. Symonds writes; "Literary style is a more a matter of sentimental emotion involuntary habits of feeling and observing constitutional sympathy with the world and men, tendencies of curiosity and liking, than of the pure intellect"[59]. Pointing out at the function of a stylist, Symonds brings into focus the subjective impressions which make indelible imprint upon the human psyche. Symonds writes; "The stylist has here to produce the desired effect by suggestions of infinite subtlety, and to present impressions made upon his sensibility"[60]. The style and stylistics of Maugham on the other hand, remain intermingled with each other.Flaubert like Maugham gives priority to art over life and shows his reaction against the contemporary concept of realism.

In his novel 'Madam Bovary' Flaubert presents the principles of aesthetics. In this regard his comment on Mme Roger De Gennetts are apt; "People think I am in love with reality though I hate it for it is out of hatred of realism that I undertook the writing of this novel"[61]. The chief aim of literature says Maugham lies inherent in its power of liberating those "Who practise it from the contigencies of life"[62]. Maugham regards greater art as transcending the tremulousness of the maundane world. Keats' 'ode to the nightingale' is such an example of poetic transcedence that elevates the poet to the ecstasy of joy and 'pleasure'. Flaubert flamboyantly makes assertion of his faith in the transcendence of art, the art which has the propensity to retrieve Man from the mundane realities of life. Flaubert firmly believes in the trancendental quality of art giving his charecter fire and brimstone to aspire for transcendence and emancipation from the mundane world. Flaubert writes; "I would like to write all that I see not as it is but transfigured[63]. F.H. Bradley's immediate experience, on the other hand, co-relates 'self- realization' with the infinite. Maugham like F. H. Bradley and Goethe too takes self-realisation to be the touchstone of transcendence. Maugham writes; "I suppose that Goethe means that man makes the most of his life when he arrives at self- realisation"[64].

Maugham delineats his 'criticism of art' on the basis of asthetic sense. Aesthetic beauty, to him, has ethical meaning in its manifestation of art. Like Flaubert Maugham artistically discerns that the function of criticism should be unconcerned with the mere pursuit of beauty. In 'The Moon and Six Pence' he defines art to be a manifestation of emotion. In Maugham's exploration of aesthetics the language emanating from the aesthetic emotion alone can communicate to Man in the midst of facing the odds of the 'real' life. Bringing into focus the inadequacies of the realistic cult of writing, Maugham writes; "art is a manifestation of emotion, and emotion speaks a language that all may understand. But I will allow that the critic who has not a practical knowledge of technique is seldom able to say anything on the subject of real value and my ignorance of painting is extreme."[65] Whereas in Eliot's "Function of Criticism" ethics and aesthetics lie ensconced not in the expression of personality but in complete abnegation of the self. Eliot's aesthetic verse limits itself to the suppression of the subjective emotions; Dorothy Richardson, in her depiction of the human psyche concentrates on the immediate experience. In Principles of Criticism, I. A. Richards, relies on the 'emotive' language of communication. In his book, 'The Foundation of Aesthetics' (1922) Richards defines beauty in terms of the effects and after-effects perceived in the audience of art. In "The Meaning of Meaning" (1923) Ogden and Richards rather give a new dimension of meaning to semantics by discriminating between symbolic use of the ethics of language in science and its 'emotive' use in poetry. Richard's 'emotive' language of poetry thus cumulatively culminates in practical criticism. (1929) like Richards, Maugham takes aesthetic art to be the supreme form of communication. Like Richards Maugham is an artist who is well versed in the art of aesthetics. 'Beauty, in Maugham's exploration of aesthetics is based on the gospel of the apocalypse. Hence in his bid to define his aesthetic stance in the outside world, he employs a syllogistic proposition to define the varied naunces of beauty. To him, it is the intermingling of knowledge, sensitiveness and imagination which alone can define the aesthetic function of beauty. Maugham writes; "Beauty is something wonderful and strange that the artist fashions out of the chaos of the world in the torment of his soul. And when he has made it, it is not given to all to know it. To recognise it you must repeat the adventure of the artist. It is a melody that he sings to you, and to hear it again in your own heart you want knowledge and sensitiveness and imagination"[66].

Beauty, says Maugham, performs ethical function by creating communication between the self and the outside world. It plays a conciliatory role between Man's nature and his business of life. "The Beauty of life", he says, "is nothing but this, that each should act in conformity with his nature and his business"[67]. Unlike Keats, Maugham is no escapist. Beauty in the realm of Keatsean poetic sensibility takes man from the mundane to the ideal. Beauty implicit in the paradox of the dark and savage passion enkindles in Man a greater reality. His characters portrayed on his dialectical canvas are enthused with aesthetic beauty to find communication and co-relation with Man's throbbing self and the environs he dwells in. Maugham defines the aesthetic value of the ugly and the beautiful by the vehicle of 'association'. It is the 'consciousness' implicit in Man which arouses feelings of hatred and admiration. James Joyce in his novel, 'Portrait of the artist as a Young Man' applies the vehicle of epiphany—the images of flow and the images of flight that create consciousness on the psycho- analytical plane. Maugham, on the other hand, applies the mechanism of 'association' with all its analogy and contrast which enables the artist to draw up a line of demarcation between the ugly and the beautiful; good and evil; ethical and unethical. Maugham writes; "All this means that association, by likeness or contrast centres largely into the aesthetic emotion. It is only association that can explain the aesthetic value of the ugly."[68] Defining the metaphysics of love, Maugham says that love devoid of the aesthetic emotion is always fraught with annihilating Man's inner urge of perceiving beauty in which aesthetic beauty plays a reconciliatory role of cohering the self and the outside world. "Love is not always blind, says Maugham, and there are few things that cause greater wretchedness than to love with all your heart someone who you know is unworthy of love,"[69]. In his exploration of metaphysics, love says Maugham thrives not on satisfaction but on impediments. Love in Maugham's domain of aesthetics can't achieve transcendence unless it becomes passion. Man in Maugham' s realm of ethics and aesthetics is obsessed with defining his aesthetic stance of life in the 'real' world. In order to live at par with the ethics of the 'self' he unhesitatingly takes the stance of relinquishing every finite object he owes. The subliminal passions enkindle in him an urge to know the unknowableness of that aspect of life what is dark, primitive and the occult. The subjective emotions in Maugham's protagonist are a devastating force that compels Man to look into the Unknown.

Maugham is a 'disinterested' observer of the 'real' life. His dialectical consciousness which is a totality of sensitiveness, knowledge and ethical imagination makes him conscious of the inadequacies of the 'real' outside world. Maugham unlike Shaw, Wells and Galsworthy is not averse to the squalor, poverty and economic deprivation instead he accepts them as they exist. For him the prevalance of squalor, poverty and sordid realities stand for the greater consciousness. With the realization that the painted veil of the 'real' world, should be seen as they are. Maugham feels himself no more averse to the squalor, and vices and poverty. For Maugham the vices, the squalor poverty and sordid realities of life get transmuted into the Whole consciousness opening up a new threshold of perceiving greater realities. This shows how the unconscious part of the human psyche too makes impact upon the human consciousness from Freud's psycho-analytical stand point. Frome who belongs to the post Freudian era, says that the instinctual patterns too seek their participation in the behavioural patterns of life. No sooner does Maugham realize that the Vice, Squalor and poverty and other sordid realities too unfold a meaning for understanding those 'impulses of the heart' than he pins his hope in the manifold inward manifestation of greater life.

Maugham is a disinterested observer of human nature. For him, the business of a writer is not to instruct but to 'please' . In 'The Summing Up' Maugham puts emphasis on the element of 'pleasure' which, to him, becomes a vehicle of communication between the disinterested 'writer' and the 'listener'. Maugham writes; "I sighed for the liberty of fiction and I thought with pleasure of the lonely reader who was willing to listen to all I had to say and with whom I could effect an intimacy that I could never hope for in the garish publicity of the theatre."[70] Maugham is at the same time critical of those writers who write to liberate their spirit of subject. A 'good' writer says Maugham is one who doesn't write to unburden his spirit of subject instead "he will take care to write only for the sake of his own peace".[71] Maugham neither believes in dialectical Materialism nor in the governance writ large by the capitalistic patterns of society. Charles Darwin in his 'Origin of Species' had materialistically believed in the survival of the fittest. Darwin delineates his theory of evolution saying that all those who are less capable of survival are subject to be extinct. But Maugham unlike Darwin regards the vices, the squalor and poverty and man's lack of survival instinct are part of the greater realities of human life. Maugham can't afford to ignore the finite objects which conform to the totality of the whole consciousness. 'Survival' for Maugham can' t be connotated in terms of the degree of the economic and materialistic developments. "The Only, survival, Maugham aesthetically rejoices, that has any value is the complete survival of the individual."[72] 'Consciousness' says Maugham is thus directly related with the survival of the individual. It is an instrument which solipsistically enables Man to deal with the pretentions and hypocrisies of the 'real' world. Consciousness to Maugham thus is a vehicle which establishes communication between the self and the environment. Eliot doesn't allow the 'turning loose of emotions to embark on a work of art. He employs objectivity by the technique of objective correlative—a series of images that constrain the subjective emotions. Maugham, unlike Eliot, concentrates on the subjective correlatives. In Maugham's delineation of a work of art, the foremost work of an artist is to interpret and develop a sense of 'association'. The dynamics of 'association' followed up by analogy and contrast, enables Maugham to enter into the aesthetic emotion. Characters thus portrayed on the canvas of Maugham's fictional art thus undergo an 'inward' process of 'association' on the basis of which they distinguish between the sacred and profane, the ugly and the beautiful. To Maugham, self-realization is the vehicle which makes man spiritually awakened to the 'new' world of 'spirits' . The ideas of association create in him a faculty of dialectics by virtue of which he enhances the area of consciousness. Thus 'association' which projects consciousness, acts as a vehicle of generating self-realization. Maugham writes;" I do not care if people are interested in me or not I have no desire to impart my knowledge, I have to others nor do I feel the need to correct them if they are wrong. You can get a great deal of entertainment out of the tedious people. If you keep your head."[73]

Maugham is a literary critic with a keen sense of objectivity. He takes the currents and cross-currents of the 'real' world to be self illusory. He looks at the squalor and poverty of the 'real' world as they are. Maugham writes; "I do not want to talk and I am very willing to listen"[74] shows how Maugham is committed to take art to be a supreme form of communication. In his another essay, 'variation on a theme' He delineates the real function of a critic. Defining what the real function of a critic is, Maugham writes; " Now I am not a critic and it is not my business to criticise."[75] Eliot manoeuvres from 'turning loose of emotions'; Maugham, on the other hand, gives priority to the expression of personality. For him self-realization alone can give transcendence to a work of art. In his remarkable essay "Variation on a theme", Maugham reiterates, "I ask you can an artist give you more or better than himself? I shall never grow tired of asserting that it is the artist's personality and that alone, what gives the work of art its enduring significance."[76] Being a disinterested observer of human nature, he appreciates multifoliate naunces of human nature that Dorothy Parker delineates in her stories. Admiring the 'heart felt woes' that she infuses in her art of story telling, Maugham writes "She presents herself to you, to take or to leave, with her pain, her laughter, her tenderness, her feeling for beauty, her ribaldry and her common sense."[77] The function of 'humour' says Maugham, is to exercise to discrepancies of human nature; "A sense of humour, says Maugham, leads you to take pleasure in the discrepancies of human nature."[78] Maugham shows his disagreement with the conventional stories which traditionally have a beginning, a middle and an end. Such "drab stories in which nothing happens"'[79] says Maugham, do not satisfy and cater to the aesthetic needs of the reader.

Maugham attributes Checkov's stories to conventional types; Chekov's stories are built upon the moral preponderance in which "writers very often apt to believe, namely that what he was best able to do was the best thing to do."[80] Such conventional stories, says Maugham, lack the propensity to grow with all their heartfelt woes of pain, and loneliness. He, on the other hand, loves to tell the stories of 'experience' which have tenacity "to tell plausible."[81] Maugham is a story teller par excellence. Unlike the conventional stories of Chekov, the stories of love, pain, loneliness and self-realization, Maugham creates, are replete with a sense of pleasure and amusement. Pleasure says Maugham is an instrument which acts as a vehicle to represent and imitate human nature in all its purple and multi-foliate shades and colours. What Maugham strikingly emphasizes is the turning loose of the aesthetic emotion. It is the expression of personality which evokes a greater reality in a work of art. The overflow of the aesthetic emotion in a work of art, says Maugham enkindles an urge to spiritualize the 'senses'. In his another essay, 'The Writer's point of view', he writes that the expression of personality with all its innate instincts plays a pivotal role in making art a proper vehicle of communication between Man and his surroundings; Maugham writes;

> "whatever he writes is the expression of personality and it is the manifestation of his innate instincts, his feelings, his experiences and his opinion"[82]

In his another essay 'creatures of circumstances', he once again reiterates that he never pretends "to be anything but a story teller"[83] whereas in 'The writers' point of view Maugham says that the "aim of the writer of fiction, I repeat, is not to instruct but to please"[84] Maugham thus believes in the suspension of disbelief in the expression of personality. The expression of personality made by virtue of the vehicle of association —defines the stance of the ugly and the beautiful; the mechanism of analogy and contrast that creates the finer perception of aesthetic beauty. Maugham in his preface to has essay, "The partial view, eloquently writes; "I am only curious to know what is in me that is disagreeable to them"[85].

Reacting against the prevalence of the conventional stories, he says that a good novelist should necessarily be a good novelist. Characters built up upon his canvas of the fictional art are what they are from within. "Fiction, says Maugham, is an art and the purpose of art is to please"[86]. Hence it is the element of pleasure that essentially makes reading enjoyable.

Maugham looks at the existence of human life with a mystical and apocalyptical insight. He finds no heirarchy in the existence of human life. He apocalyptically finds colour, beauty, comeliness and hope in the 'creatures of circumstances'. The vivid spectrum of dialectical perspective thus streamlines the scientific and evolutionary culmination of life with the aesthetic discipline of life. The dialectical method applied by Maugham can spiritualize the "Senses". Maugham shows his bewilderment at the stupefying effect of the colossal growth of intellect upon man in the post modern era. The dialectical consciousness envisaged by Maugham thus suspends the disbelief that the 'senses' are a stumbling block to the mystical and spiritual realization of human life. Maugham thus naturalises the ever-widening consciousness—scientific evolutionary, economic and existential at every level of time. Thus the art of aesthetic emotion is thus a palatable force to adjust the ever widening gyres of consciousness with the aesthetic mainstream of life in order to present the whole being of man with all his potentialities inherent in him.

Somerset Maugham's characters remain entrapped into the tentacles of human bondage. Man has been shown caught up into the orgy of savage passions as he has propensity to be an outcome of his own being. Man's innate urge to define his 'self in the strange world makes him irresistibly caught up into the abyss of loneliness. The tentacles of human bondage are thus directly related with Man's incessant search for emancipation from the vortex of suffering and loneliness. Man' says Somerset Maugham, falls prey to the pitfalls of temptation, gullibility and licentiousness. Hence the dialectical perspective alone is feasible for attaining freedom from the state of human bondage. What Somerset Maugham dialectically argues is to identify various areas of human bondage which menacingly put obstacle to the wholesome growth of man's 'being'. What he basically envisages is that man's ardent dream of attaining emancipation will go on to persist in society unless man evolves the faculty of ratiocinating those various forms of human bondage which cause the maladies like alienation, root-lessness, disorganisation and above all spiritual sickness. Hence by applying the doctrine of dialecticism Maugham identifies various facets of bondage which make man immensely suffer in the modern world. It can however be said that Maugham's dialectics of freedom is something akin to Shaw's theory of life-force. By placing man on the canvas of the dialectical art Maugham explores the conundrum of human existence in which man irritrievably finds himself a prisoner into the cloister of the 'self'.

References

1. Quoted by Arnold Toynbee, Hellenism, edited by Gilbert Murray, Sir George Clark, The Home University library of Modern Knowledge, p. 7, ed., 1958.
2. *Ibid.*, p.7.
3. *Ibid.*, p. 13.
4. *Ibid.*, p. 14.
5. Philip Lee Ralph, The story of civilisation : A Study of the History of the Western people, Comet Books, Collins, ed., 1957, p. 9.
6. Arnold Toynbee, Hellenism, p. 15.
7. *Ibid.*, p. 15.
8. Arnold Toynbee, Faith of a Historian, edited by Sisir Kumar Ghose, Bhartiya Vidya Bhawan, Bombay, ed., 1967, p. 11.
9. Philip Lee Ralph, The history of civilisation; "A study of the history of the Western People, p. 52.
10. *Ibid.*
11. *op.cit.*
12. V. Brodov; India Philosophy in Modern Times, Progress Publishers, Moscow, ed., 1984, p. 21.
13. Oscar Wilde, The Picture of Dorian Gray, Wordsworth classics, ed., 1993, p. 35.

14. Quoted by Dorothy Parker; *The Portable*, New York, The Viking Press, ed., 1962. p. 14.
15. W. Somerset Maugham; "The Writer's point of view", London, National Book League, The Cambridge University Press, ed., 1951, p. 13.
16. Oscar Wilde, The Picture of Dorian Gray, p. 104.
17. W. Somerest Maugham, The writer's point of view, p. 17.
18. *Ibid.*
19. *Ibid.*, p. 176.
20. *Op.cit.*.
21. W. Somerset Maugham; "Of human bondage", with a digression on the art of fiction, (an address by William Somerset Maugham), Norwood Editions, ed., 1978, p. 9.
22. Philip Sydney, An Apology for Poetry.
23. W. Somerset Maugham, Of Human Bondage, pp. 356-357.
24. W. Somerset Maugham, The Razor's Edge, William Heinemann Ltd., Octopus Book Ltd., London, 1979, p. 340.
25. Somerset Maugham. The Writer's Point of View, p., 13.
26. *Op.cit.*
27. Philip Sydney; "An Apology for poetry."
28. W. Somerset Maugham; The Writer's Point of View, London, Published for Book League, The Cambridge University Press, ed., 1951, p. 13.
29. P.G. Wodehouse; Uncle Fred: An Ominous, Penguin Books, ed., 1987, p. i.
30. William Somerset Maugham; Preface, Heinemann, Octopus, Martin Seeker and Warburg, London, ed., 1979, p. 28.
31. Walter Allen, The English Novel; "A Short Critical History, Penguin Books, ed., 1954, p. 15.
32. *Ibid.*, p. 15.
33. *Ibid.*, p. 16.
34. Bertrand Russell, Mysticism and Logic, Unwin Books, ed., 1963, p. 26.
35. W. Somerset Maugham, "The Partial View", p. 43.
36. *Op.cit.*
37. Oscar Wilde, The Picture of Dorain Gray, p. 274.
38. W.B. Yeats; "The Second Coming", Palgrave's Golden

Teasury, selected by John Press, Oxford University Press, Delhi, Bombay, Madras, ed., 1988, p. 424.

39. Jean Paul Satre; "The artist and his conscious Reader", Caroline shredes, Harry Fine Stone, Micheal Shaugn, Macmillon, Publishing Co., Inc, New York, ed., 1974, p. 438.
40. T.S. Eliot; Selected Poetry, Faber and Faber, London, Boston, ed., 1980, p. 32.
41. Ebenstein William; Political thought in perspective, McGraw-Hill Book Company, Inc., New York, Toronto, London, ed., 1957, p. 273.
42. *Ibid.*, p. 273.
43. Nirad C. Chaudhuri, A passage to England, An Orient Paperback, p. 25.
44. *Ibid.*, p. 25.
45. T. S. Eliot, The Wasterland, Selected poems, Faber and Faber, London, Boston, ed., 1980, p. 65.
46. *Ibid.*, p. 83
47. Mathew Arnold, "On the Modern Element in literature", several essays, edited by G. F. J. Cumberledge, Oxford University Press, ed., 1952, p. 89.
48. *Ibid.*, p. 89.
49. *Ibid.*, p. 89.
50. *Ibid.*, p. 89.
51. *Ibid.*, p. 89.
52. *Op.cit.*
53. Mathew Arnold; " The choice of subjects in poetry", English Critical Essays, selected and edited by Edmund Jones, Oxford University Press, Delhi, ed., 1971, p. 322.
54. *Op.cit.*
55. Mathew Arnold; "Modern Element in Art," Several Essays, p.90.
56. A Clutton-Brock, "What is art ?" several essays, p. 106.
57. *Ibid.*, p. 108.
58. *Ibid.*
59. J.A. Symonds; “Personal style”, several essays, p. 102.
60. *Ibid.*, pp. 102-103.
61. Arnold Isenberg; “Aesthetics and the theory of criticism”, the University of Chicago Press, Chicago, London, ed., 1973, p. 4.

62. Brombert Victor; The novels of Flaubert: A study of themes and techniques, Princeton, New Jersy, Princeton University Press ed., 1966, p. 5.
63. Quoted by Arnold Isenberg, Aestheticism and the theory of criticism" p. 5.
64. W. Somerset Maugham; "The Summing up, Pocket Books", New York, ed. 1967, p. 207.
65. W. Somerset Maugham, The Moon and Six Pence, Penguin Books Ltd., Middle Sex England, Ed., 1970, p. 6.
66. *Ibid.*, p. 72.
67. W. Somerset Maugham, The Summing Up, Pocket Books, New York, ed. 1967, p. 230
68. *Ibid.*, p. 222.
69. *Ibid.*, p. 227.
70. *Ibid.*, p. 114.
71. *Ibid.*, p. 134.
72. *Ibid.*, p. 204.
73. *Ibid.*, p. 48
74. *Ibid.*
75. W. Somerset Maugham, "Variation on a theme", Dorothy Parker, "The portable", New York, The Viking Press, ed., 1962, p. 14.
76. *Ibid.*, pp. 17-18.
77. *Ibid.*, p. 18.
78. W. Somerset Maugham, 'The Summing Up', p. 49.
79. W. Somerset Maugham, Creatures of Circumtances, The Sun Dial Press, Garden City, New York, ed., 1948, p. 5
80. *Ibid.*, p. 5.
81. *Ibid.*, p. 6.
82. W. Somerset Maugham, The Writer's point of view, p. 13.
83. W. Somerset Maugham, creatures of circumtances, p. 6.
84. W. Somerset Maugham, The Writer's point of view, p. 13.
85. W. Somerset Maugham, The Partial View, p. VIII.
86. W. Somerset Maugham, "Of Humann Bondage" (With digression on the art of fiction p. 9.

3

Maugham and the Contemporary Literature

Somerset Maugham is a writer of considerable literary and fictional art. For him 'home is where the heart is'. Maugham solipsistically finds solace in the sustenance of the soul. He dialectically looks into the rhyme and reason of spiritual emptiness ascertaining how the modern life splits up man pushing him into the endless labyrinth of alienation from the mainstream of human life. Maugham's dialectical method of analyzing the substance of the mind, enables man to grow human relationships in which the interplay of humanistic, ethical and aesthetic values help create a harmonious living. Maugham too much relies on the Naturalistic ethics while opening up new horizons of freedom. Commenting on Maugham's emphasis on the naturalistic writing Walter Allen writes; "Too much self knowledge is probably not good for an artist, and for the most part Maugham has been content to work in a very narrow range of subject and character, without any compensating quality of style to make up for it"[1]. Maugham's preoccupation with the depiction of loneliness, gathers momentum from both the ethical and aesthetic aspirations of life. He dialectically probes man's alienation and comes to bring into focus the factors responsible for man's alienation from the mainstream of life. The Wastelanders says T. S. Eliot, are a spiritually disorganised generation. Shaw in his numerous plays emphasizes man's need to strike a balance between humanistic urges and the institutions that push man into endless trammels of loneliness. Being a realist, Shaw exposes the prevalence of social evils and the taboos which he regards them as a real stumbling block to Man's emancipation from human bondage. Eugene Marchbanks leaves Morell's house concealing within his heart a better secret. The 'heart of the matter' he carries within his 'self' is not to be unfolded before the outside world, basically shows how Shaw like Somerset Maugham and Arnold Bennet relies on the evocativeness of the throbbing self. Shaw and Maugham sharing their anguish that man needs to be retrieved from the inclemence of human bondage, shows their concern at the colossal growth of the mechanistic world which corrodes man from within. In 'Of human bondage' Philip overwhelmingly looks at the senility of growing urbanization and finds himself in need of a foothold to define his 'self at par with the ethics of the 'soul'. Arnold Bennet in his master-piece novel 'The old wives' Tale', artistically, explores the conflict between 'provincialism' and growing unbanization.

Both provincialism and the cult of urbanisation, says Bennet, are the two inseparable integrals of the human evolution. Bennet presents the landscape of the puritan life and the unshakable tranquility inherent in the ethics of 'provinciality'. Bennet writes; "It is England in little, lost in the midst of England, unsung by searchers after the extreme; perhaps occasionally somewhat sore at this neglect, but now proud in the instinctive cognizance of its representative features and traits!"[2] Constance who happens to be aghast at the growth of commercialism, remains indifferent to her 'house' of provinciality. She revels in identifying herself with the ethics of provinciality. Going beyond 'Bursley' would embroil the apple cart of her life making her tranquility upside down. Unlike Sophia, Constance is averse to the idea of visiting the outskirts which is not 'Bursely'. It is the nostalgia of staying at 'home' that makes Constance exercise her liberty. Sophia unlike Constance yields to her instincts living a life of experience. The life of provinciality and experience thus presents a complete picture of life on the canvas of Arnold's fictional art.. Sophia Bains like Philip, is necessarily conscious of the mettle of the 'self'. Her elopement with Gerald skies opens up for her a new life of experience and enterprise. In spite of being forsaken by her husband in the midst she displays heroic and masculine endeavour in not retreating to Bursley and goes on to live facing the odds of life all alone. Her refusal to give allowance to chirac and Napier, shows how fidelity to conforming to the ethics of the soul is more important to her than yielding to her impulse. "I can not be bothered with all the sort of thing. It is not worth while. What does it lead to ? Is not life complicated enough without that? No, no! I will stay as I am. At any rate I know what I am in for, as things are I"[3] There is nothing dilemma nor is any partial and half-hearted assertion of her spirited aesthetic vision in getting her back to the business of Bursley. Her resolution to live what ever she is, provides her the basic impetus to achieve transcendence and retain her basic identity she remains wrapped up with. She returns to the Anna of the five Towns with the assertion that; "She was conscious of an immeasurable superiority to him, for she was conscious of the freedom of a strong mind."[4]

Somerset Maugham's characters like Philip, Larry, Kitty and Liza Lambeth are not a spent-up force, instead the life of physicality and ordeal they are made to undergo, open up the threshold of entering into the realm of spiritual regeneration. Somerset Maugham through his dialectical art, presents a cosmic vision of life in which his artistic vision is applied for streamlining the bodily and spiritual experiences. Sophia like Philip wouldn't accept which is less than the ethics of her soul while undergoing the ordeal of experience. As to Philip feels the need to invent a way out to catering to both the ethical and aesthetic aspirations. Being essentially conscious that her husband has betrayed and forsaken her in the midst, she has her affirmation to live at par with the doctrine of the self. She does not bear any; "disdain from sense of injured merit"[5]. While exercising her freedom, she feels herself spirited enough to exercise her freedom by sticking to her self. Maugham's characters are thus fired up with the effervescence of life complying with the ethics of the soul. Constance's resolution of not going beyond the provincial 'Bursley' is thus linked up with her own idea of the perservance of identity. Sophia Bains exults life amidst all its uncertainties and unprecedentedness which it mysteriously unfolds itself to the real world. It needs to be seen with objectivity whether Maugham admired Bennet. Anthony Curtis in this regards expressing his opinion on the fictional art of Bennet says that Maugham constantly admired Bennet's 'The old wives' Tale' when it appeared in 1908 but he at the same time "always regarded Bennet with somewhat contempt"[6]. Commenting on the art of Arnold Bennet, Somerset Maugham's writes;' He was cocksure and sumptuous and was rather common'[7]. Summing up his ideas on the art of Arnold Bennet, Maugham writes; 'I don't say this depreciatinglingly but as I might say that some one was short and fat'[8]. Somerset Maugham like Flaubert essentially concentrates on the aesthetic aspirations. Throwing light on Flaubert's "evocativeness of carnality and orgiastic violence, says, Bombert, are, however bought up with an irremediable sense of sadness and futility"[9]. On the other hand, Huxley says Atkins John was "the antithesis of Lawrence"[10]. The former says Atkins was "rational, tolerant and scientific"[11] in temperament whereas later was "instinctive, condemnatory and apocalyptic'[12]. The voice of the self says Huxley is a cry of wilderness in the Brave New world. The loss of individuality operating in the Brave New world, entwines man into the endless trammels of frustration. Huxley opines that cessation of individuality can be extirpated by the verbiage of vitalism. Huxley in the Brave New world writes; "And, of course, whenever the masses seized political power, it was happiness rather that truth and beauty that mattered."[13]

D. H. Lawrence like Maugham emphasizes the need of paying heed to the revival of 'sexual instinct' which he dialectically opines, too plays a crucial role in spiritualising the senses and in satisfying man's credo of passions, in order to revitalise the spirits' of the attainment of freedom in every sphere of life. In 'Of human bondage', Maugham brings into focus those instinctual patterns and emotion of multitude which remain implicit in human nature. Nature in Mildred manifests its palatable power to upturn the applecart of the realistic society. She is no coy mistress; she is pert and dare-devil but ironically lacks the vision and perspicacity to have empathy enough to cater to Philip's aesthetic and metaphisical aspirations. Like Robinson Crusoe, Philip is seen pitiably struggling against the odds of Nature. The metaphysics of love as depicted by Maugham knows no reason. Characters projected on Maughams' dialectical art, do not remain caught up in a dilemma nor do they devise parallel ways and means to live up their life with a renewed sense of compromise. Maugham's metaphysics of love moves round the basic identity they have from within. Maugham dialectically argues that the fury of passions ensconced in the cloister of the self, has a propensity to thwart and restrain the spiritual discord projected by mechanics of the real world. Maugham like Syng and Sean O' Casey came to realize that realism was no longer an instrument of projecting the whole emerging picture of man in the modern world. Mildred is the antithesis of Ann Whitefield. Nature makes Mildred an object of captivating Philip to create in him an urge to aesthetically feel the fury of the dark elemental passion which plays a mystical role in making man conscious of his self and identity. On the other hand Ann Whitefield who assumes to play the role of nature ensnares Tanner to create a better human race. This conflict of will in Shaw's realm of drama, intends to create a better society. Maugham is a disillusioned realist who aesthetically saw that the instrument of realism was inadequate to fulfil the dream of attaining emancipation in every sphere of life. Therefore Maugham by applying the machanics of his dialectical art, wants to emancipate art from the 'realistic' convention of writing. Lawrence who was well aware of the monstrosity of the scientific and the industrial revolutions, on the other hand, comes to realize how they are untenable to sustain the human and spiritual values. In 'The plumed serpent (1926), the primitive has been contrasted with the modern. Kate on the instinctual plane hates the bullfight; "Human cowardice and beastliness, a smell of blood, a nauseaus whiff of bursten bowels! She turned her face away"[14]. A conflict of will thus operates in Lawrence's novel. Lawrence who was averse to the abnormal growth of intellect, essentially believes in the wisdom of blood-intimacy. Kate says to Don Raman; "Oh! isn't human life horrible! she carried. Every human being exerting his will all the time even other people, and over himself and nearly always self-righteous!"[15] In 'The Lost Girl' Alvina Houghton feels her self aghast at the lack-lustre and the sordid realities of the mechanical world. She rebels against the mechanical and the spiritually sterile world which to her is not even worth-living. She feels that it is better for her to be slave girl than to be part of the 'mechanical routine of the modern work'. Alvina like Julia rebells against the mechanical way she has to display her pantomime in the illusive world of the 'theatre'. Man-woman relationship, says Lawrence, has gone out of sync in the modern-industrial society. In Lawrence's novel, 'The Lost Girl' she has no way out to come out of the mechanical society; She tetters and totters against the callousness of the mechanical society she finds herself ensnared in; "She rebelled with all her backbone against the word job. Even the substitutes, employment or word were detestable, unbearable. Emphatically she did not want to work for a wage... The most vulgar, sordid and humiliating of all forms of slavery : so mechanical. For better to be a slave girl outright, in contact with all the whims and impulses of a human being than serve mechanical routine of modern work"[16]. Keeping in view of the spiritual sterility caused by the advent of the industrial and the mechanical society, Lawrence seeks for intellectual independence. Lawrence's 'Women in Love' is thus a novel of ideas projected in conflict with the new morality of science each other. Birkin argues for a new sexual morality in order to remove the constraints operating on the diverse social and cultural planes. Tolstoy unlike Lawrence writes with all his moral compunction to create his world of emancipation. Tolstoy's characters are pre-occupied with the resolution of being stock characters of the moral and the spiritual order. Alexey Alexandrovitch says to Anna; "To enter into all the details of your feelings I have no right, and besides, I regard that as useless and even harmful; began Alexey Alexandrovitch, Ferreting in one soul, one often ferrets out something that might have lain there unnoticed. Your feelings are an affair of your own conscience; but I am in duty bound to you, to myself, and to God, to point out to your duties. Our life has been joined, not by man, but by God"[17] Levin too, in 'Anna Karenina' feels himself pre-occupied with the moral compunction, on the other hand takes reason to be essential for cultivating belief in the apocalyptical order. Levin basically is aware of the inherent dangers of 'knowing'. But at the same time he realizes that the 'reason' in him takes him to the terrace of the apocalypse. To Levin 'reason' has a two fold function. Levin feels that "without knowing what I am and why I am here, life's impossible; and that I can't know, and so I can't live".[18] Tolstoy explicates the conundrum of the human existence and says that human nature can't achieve transcendence unless Man firmly believes in the ecclesiastical order. Tolstoy is apprenhesive of the negative implications of attaining 'knowledge, and reason' which to him is something akin to committing trangression. Levin undergoes the conflict operating between knowledge and belief. Reason in Tolstoy's exploration of Human Nature embroils Man in dilemma. Reason had brought him to doubt, and prevented him from seeing what he ought to do and what he ought not. It is conscience not reason which is the guardian angel in Tolstoy's exploration of the apocalypse. He was always conscious of the presence of 'the infallible judge' in his soul that prevented him from being astray. In Tolstoy's concept of freedom, conflict between reason and conscience remains operating through out the gamut of the human experience. When he did not think, but simply lived, he was continually aware of the presence of an infallible judge in his soul, determining which of the two possible causes of action was the better, and which was the worse, and as soon as he did not act rightly, he was once aware of it. On the other hand, Lawrence was conscious of the monstrosity of the mechanical society, symbolically creates an urge for attaining liberation through rythms, patterns and images. Ursula is every woman who frantically searches for emancipation from the bondage of sex and social constraints. In 'Rainbow', Ursula is betrayed by Anton but she optimistically doesn't yield to despair. She optimistically percieves the rainbow which symbolizes liberation from the bondage of sex, social constraints. Atkins John writes; "Lawrence's most valuable gift was not his worship of instinct and dark forces, which could easily degenerate into Diabolism but his sensitiveness towards nature and his insistence that never attempt to cut links between him and it"[19]. Aldous Huxley on the other hand, was deeply aware of the intricacies of degenerating and dehumanizing attributes of the 'Brave New world'. Huxley made no secret of the dangers inherent deeply steeped in hedonism. Huxley writes; "I like to see pictures from which nature has been completely banished."[20]. Huxley brings into focus the "pictures which are exclusively the product of the human mind."[21]. In the Brave New world, (1932) Huxley exposes the inculcation of the scientific and the materalistic growth of society which has proneness to cease individual integrity. In Huxley's Brave New world, Man has been shown bewildering in search of a world where he could aspire for the re-integration of the self. In his another novel 'Eyeless Gaza' (1938). Huxley stresses the need to cultivate the philosophy of the universal love. Maugham instead, moves up from the personal to the universal plane striking a balance between ethical and aesthetic aspirations. Liza is fired up with the aspiration of coming up the banality of the mundane world. Larry feels himself lacerated at the disaster and devastation caused by the resurgence of the war which in turn annihilates his prospects of attaining happiness. The devastation caused by the inclemence of war makes him undergo a change of heart. He is no more exilirated at the conventional wisdom of attaining 'happiness' with both his hands. He no more feels the need to run after 'happiness' which can't even give sustenance to asthetic and metaphysical sensibility. Larry shows his dissent at the success; glamour and glory that society gives to man in lieu of his obedience to the conventional ethics. As Maugham is a rebel par excellence, the colossal growth of the mechanical society makes him conscious of the impulse that puts obstacles to human aspirations man has had. Lear, in an identical way cries with utmost despair;

> "O, Reason not the need! Our basest beggars
> Are in the poorest thing superfluous.
> Allow not nature more than nature needs,

Man's life is cheap as beast's.

Thou art a lady; If only to go warm were gorgeous,

Why, nature needs not what thou gorgeous wear'st"[22]

This shows how the obedience to the conventional ethics makes man embroiled into the tentacles of human bondage. Unlike Lear, Larry seeks his freedom in imposing self- mortification. Kitty grows conscious of the onslaught of loneliness that seizes her soul up in black despair. An urge to come out of the state of bondage makes her entharalled with sensation. She is dragged into the plague-striken city wherein she has nothing to communicate with. The problem of loneliness on account of her failure to establish her communion with her husband, embroils her life from within. Cordelia too overwhelmingly experiences the evanescence of the factors responsible for making convulsion of the moral order. The economic factor in the new mechanical society wherein man runs meaninglessly to the illusive life, Maugham says, no more brings sustenance to make their life harmonious. Maugham thus emphasizes the need to find a way out to a harmonious life of flesh and spirit in the modern spiritually ailing society. The two stoic philosophers, Epicetus (circa A. D., 50-120) and Marcus Aurelius (A.D. 121-180) take reason to be the principal guiding force. Man says Epicetus has been bestowed with his rational faculty to apply what is within his power. Marcus Aurelius similarly argues that the rational self seeks perfection and tranquility in doing what is just.

"Seek not, says the stoic slave philosopher Epicetus, that the things which happen should happen as you wish; but wish the things which happen to be as they are, and you will tranquil flow of life"[23]. Kalidasa in his play, 'Sakuntala' too explores the stoic landscape of resignation and surrender where every-thing is made ensconced into self-fulfilment. The ascetics portrayed in Kalidasa's 'Sakuntala' artistically discern evocativeness of the self in the stoic world. They make the king aware of the stoic life they live;

"By seeing how the ascetics' holy rites
are free of all hindrance,
you will realize how much
Your bow-scarred arm protects"[24].

Priyamvada who dwells along with her friends, Anusuya and Sakuntala into the confines of the stoic hermitage share their stoic life with one another. "Priyamvada : Sakuntala; dearest, we've watered all the summer-flowering trees. Let's water the ones that have finished flowering, and store up merit for ourselves by a disinterested action. Sakuntala: Priyamvada, that's a lovely idea.

Again she acts watering the trees."[25] To say that the primitive, stoic and the tragic land-scapes Maugham paints is tinged with cynicism, doesn't have justification in the sense that the characters Maugham paints have tenacity to rejoice their life with all its manifold and exequisite colours. Maugham's characters therefore essentially have the tenacity and verbiage to make all out affort for sustaning their self in the mechanical society. Philip can't repose faith in the success-oriented life. Kitty who grows conscious of the onslaught of loneliness, yields to the conventional morality. Her marriage to Walter ironically gives no relief to her spirits. Feeling herself seized up with the frenzy of her soul, she aspires for hope, comliness and beauty in her renunciation of the mundane world. Philip too can't even opt for a way out other than seeing a ray of hope in Mildred. Mildred makes no attempt to take into account the factors responsible for Philip's anguish and his disillusionment with the modern world. The metaphysics of love in Maugham's dialectics thus operates both at ethical and aesthetic planes. Unlike Candida Mildred remains indifferent to Philip's aesthetic perception of life. She fails to address the threat to the self impinged by the colossal growth of the mechanical world. The artistic failure in Mildred is palatable enough to make Philip ensconced in black despair. The projection of 'hyacynth-girl', in Eliot's 'The wasteland', exposes the profanation of love. 'Nymphs', are no more found at the embankment of the Thames, symbolically points out at the drying up of the spiritual values. Unlike Eliot Maugham evocatively shows the sombre world of materialism in which hedonistic pleasure is taken to be the wholesome virtue. Maugham hence dialectically argues to identify the areas of darkness which put up the human aspirations in conflict with the conventional ethics. Maugham is basically conscious of the factors shaping up the identity of Man. Huxley like Eliot elaborates how man suffocatively finds himself prisoner in the scientific paradise. Man says Huxley runs after the hedonistic pleasure in the Brave New World. Maugham on the other hand opines that a mere puritanical approach to life is no answer to attainment of emancipation; merely taming the untamed wild and violent emotions and that avoiding pleasure, brings no spiritual fulfilment to human life. Maugham unlike Huxley emphasizes the dialectical approach to rationalise the humanistic urges for opening up new horizons of freedom. Oscar Wilde in his novel, 'The Picture of Dorian Gray', explores the naunces of the aesthetic art. Dorian Gray like Macbeth is partially made aware of the mystery of beauty. Dorian Gray who takes beauty to be 'a province' doesn't ironically know the reasons behind Man's proneness to the susceptibilities of impulse. Wilde like Maugham probes the factors responsible for bringing about disintegration of the body and soul. 'Beauty' comes up on Gray as a 'revelation'. Basil bares his heart, puts too much of his soul into the picture of Dorian Gray and makes it a real work of art in flesh and blood. Lord Henry on the other hand emphasizes the need of applying the logic of passions; "But it appeared to Dorian Gray that the true nature of the senses had never been understood and that they had remained savage and animal merely because the world had sought to stare them into submission or to kill them by pain, instead of aiming at making them elements of a new spirituality, of which a fine instinct for beauty was to be the dominant characteristic."[26] Oscar Wilde thus points out at the dangers inherent in the blind "worship of the senses"[27] that leads man to dissipation of the body and soul. Oscar Wilde like Maugham aesthetically argues to conform to the aesthetic philosophy emphasising the need to cleanse the soul through the senses. As Dorian Gray, remains unaware of the danger inherent in the adoration of the 'senses' he surreptitiously falls prey to the innuendo of temptation and allows himself to be ensnared into despair and loneliness. Both Wilde and Maugham believe that Man can't be 'happy' and 'good' at the same time. Wilde writes; "To be good is to be in harmony with one's self," he replied, touching the thin stem of his glass with his pale, fine-pointed fingers. "Discord is to be forced to be in harmony with others."[28] Dorian Gray undergoes the process of condescension and realizes the need to be spiritually cleansed making confession of the basic fact that "senses, no less than the soul, have their spiritual mysteries to reveal"[29]. 'Beauty' in Wilde's exploration of aesthetics corrodes into the being of man from within. Dorian feels himself aesthetically swept off into the endless throes of loneliness. Maugham sharing Wilde's anguish at Man's being struck by 'beauty' and stresses the need to deal with the fury of passion with the logic of the dialectics of freedom. Maugham's characters don't get condescended and consumed; They aren't hence a mere spent up force. Shaw in his play 'Candida' laughs at the conventional wisdom with which man-woman relationship is dealt with. To him the economic factor and its concept of self-reliance for carving out man-woman relationship is flimsy and impervious. Morel unlike Candida, takes the economic self sufficiency to be the crucial factor for reaping happiness in the matrimonial life. Eugene March Banks, goes into the dark with his aesthetics concealing a better secret. Both Candida and Philip are logistically apprehensive of the romance of the condescension taking place at the physical and psychic planes. Love in Maugham's world doesn't take man to the illusive and Platonic world instead it makes man dialectically conscious enough to streamline the fury of passion with the rationale of the logistics in order to prevent man from the illusive life of realism. Maugham thus dialectically identifies those areas of darkness which inculcate human bondage. The conflict operating between man and the conventional society says Maugham, puts man up in the chains. All human aspirations of freedom sought in terms of both the socialistic and capitalistic revolutions, says Maugham don't in realistic terms, emancipate Man from the tentacles of human bondage. Nor does the Lasezfare open up flood gates of freedom on the aesthetic and spiritual planes. Maugham's dialectical philosophy thus cuts across both the socialistic and capitalistic ways of living. Maugham thus dialectically argues at length to streamline the fury of passions in order to invent a new cult of spirituality in which both the ethical and aesthetic dimensions of life remain ensconced.

Great art as depicted by Maugham is not merely ephermal. Nor is it "a transient refreshment"[30]. Instead it is something which caters to the soul's self-attainment. F.H. Bradley equates it with self-fulfilment. It justifies itself both by its immediate enjoyment and by its discipline of the innermost beings"[31]. Eliot in his remarkable essay, 'Frontiers of criticism', clarifies that understanding and enjoyment go hand in hand evoking a unified sensibility but Maugham's concept of art lies embedded to his dialectical-principle. Reposing his faith in the dialectical art, Maugham holds almost a different dimension of discipline which is "not distinct from enjoyment, but by reason of it"[32]. The great art as delineated by Maugham, "transforms the soul into the permanent realization of values extending beyond its former self."[33] In 'The Moon and Six pence' "Art, has been defined as a, manifestation of emotion, and emotion speaks a language that all may understand. But I will allow that the critic who has not a practical knowledge of technique is seldom able to say any thing on the subject of real value, and my ignorance of painting is extreme."[34] The work of art on the other hand, circumscribes Croce is always 'internal' and what is called 'external' to him, is beyond the frontiers of great art. In this respects Franz Boas points out at "the two fold source of artistic effect, the one based on form alone, the other on ideas associated with form"[35].

Taking into account Franz Boas' two fold artistic effect, Arnold Isenberg deals with the basic forms of perception, meaning and the subject matter of art. Aesthetic theory, says Isenberg, then, "must establish the existence of interpretations which are not fundamentally influential and productive"[36]. Elaborating the aesthetic theory Isenberg says that the immediate can not be identified with the sensuous. Isenberg further says that "the aesthetic theory will now have to show how meanings admitted as legitimate, can be renounced with the conditions that define the aesthetic experience as such otherwise it must continue to fluctuate between intolerable extremes, where the field is either reduced to the field of sense, with undue restriction of its scope or assimilated to a mode of cognition, with consequent impairment of the very marks which delimit the aesthetic"[37]. "Hence the aesthetic fact, says Isenberg, is complete in aesthetic elaboration of impression"[38]. As the aesthetic experience emanates from perception for its own sake, Santayana emphasizes the need to conforming to the aesthetic experience. It is in this context, Santayana defines language as a "symbol for intelligence rather than a stimulus to sense"[39]. Therefore Isenberg asserts that "content"[40] is essential for the aesthetic experience. He further elaborates the function of the aesthetic experience arguing that "it is by no means essential that content be supplied by sense"[41]. "Language, which is regarded as, a symbol for intelligence, to Isenberg, is an instrument for dealing with things other than symbols themselves, with a world vastly transcending the scope of immediate attention"[42]. For Flaubert the highest and the purest form of literature lies inherent in "the highest and purest pleasure of literature is its power to liberate those who practice it from the contingencies of life"[43]. Flaubert's assertion of faith in a work of art on the other hand is an indirect "outcome of the hatred of realism"[44]. Flaubert thus interprets human life in terms of 'consumption'. "Life, says Flaubert, is not fought and lost but spent"[45]. Elaborating his concept of aesthetic experience Flaubert writes; "I would like to write all that I see not as it is but transfigured"[46]. Great art, on the other hand in Maugham's exploration of dialecticism, adds "introversion to the extroversion with which the creative instinct, is inexorably associated"[47]. Balzac explicates the conundrum of human life from the psycho-physical aspects. Sharing Maugham's anguish of unfolding the self, Balzac has a flair of exploring the being of Man. Man while living the instinctual patterns of life, says Balzac, has a propensity to face bewilderment at not finding space to define the self in the bizarre real world, enkindles in him, a creative force, the power of evocating both knowledge and imagination. The faculty of imagination is a yardstick through which he looks into and surveys the natural processes of social life. Commenting on Balzac's art of characterisation Baudlair writes; "All Balzac's characters are gifted with the sad ordour of life that animated himself. All his fictions art as dreams. Every mind is a weapon loaded to the muzzle with will. The very scullions have genius"[48]. In Maugham's fictional art, the creative forces are powerful enough to transmute reality into transcedance. Maugham writes; "The basic concepts not only appealed to my dramatic insight, they filled me besides with a very delectable sense of freedom"[49]. Oscar wilde too aesthetically explains how the aesthetic beauty comes into conflict with intellect. Dorain Gray to whom 'beauty' comes as a 'revelation' becomes aware of its inherent charm which makes him yield to his 'senses'. Dorian Gray who momentarily grows conscious of his own diminishing beauty, yields to the 'senses' without knowing how mysteriously the sudden revelation of beauty would make him astray to the world of experience. Maugham's characters after undergoing the songs of experience thus get spiritually cleansed and open up horizons for coming up the mundane life. In 'A portrait of the Artist as a young man' Joyce draws up identical experiences of cleansing the soul through the senses. Stephen Dedalus gets pandied and comes across the trauma inculcated by the conventional ethics. "O, if not the eagles will come and pluck out his eys"[50], is excruciating enough to traumatise his senses. Undergoing from one experience to another, Joyce employs the technique of epiphany; the images of flow and the images of flight to present a complete picture of the being of man. Stephen Dedalus after passing through the experience of physicality, sees freedom in resorting to "silence, exile and cunning. Lawrence writes; "I will not serve that in which I no longer believe, whether it call itself my home my fatherland, or my church; and I will try to express myself in some mode of life or art as freely as I can and as wholly as I can, using my defence the only arms I allow myself to use—silence, exile, and cunning"[51]. To Oscar Wilde, adjusting one's 'individualism' with the standard of one's age, causes discord and disharmony with 'others'. Wilde writes; "Besides, individualism has really the higher aim. Modern morality consists in accepting the standard of one's age. I consider that for any man of culture to accept the standard of his age is a form of grossest immorality"[52]. T. S. Eliot on the other hand in his essay, 'Tradition and Individual Talent', explains how an artist comes across the motley colours of values of one's age. Eliot opines that the function of artist is not to find new emotions instead he argues for the re-adjustment of the past with the existing order. Disagreeing with Eliot's interpretation of tradition and individual talent, Maugham on the other hand concentrates on solipsism. Oscar Wilde equates it with 'individualism'.

The concept of emancipation Lawrence explores in his novels is an intermingling of the mystical, aesthetic and realistic vision. His novels are relevant in the nse that they embody a transcedental reality which has power enough to sweep man out of his horror-stricken life of the society he lives in. He therefore sincerely argues to restore the dissipated human values. Lawrence rejects the world of science which makes man indifferent to his eternal part he possess within. As such he powerfully argues for a new decent society wherein every man has an opportunity to live his own life. This shows that D. H. Lawrence sincerely feels the wisdom of 'blood' intimacy which is, to him, the only touchstone of measuring the 'truth and freedom'. Lawrence staunchly believes that intellect alone can't create spiritual consolation and a balanced life of body and soul. He therefore, feels that intellectual evolution gives rise to the dehumanizing forces and distortion of feeling-pattern of man. Lawrence never believes in the utopian world which takes man to the scientific and technological progresses he has achieved so far. The scientific and technological developments, says Lawrence, have pushed man to the brink of materialism and the ghastliness of the modern civilization. As such the World saw the two World Wars that brought about infinite suffering to man. It is this monstrosity, callousness and compartmentalization of the society that compel Lawrence to write against such negative intellectual power. He therefore retrogrades to the primitiveness of life which has inexhaustible zest and vigour to restore the disorganised human condition. In order to retrieve man from the 'smog', 'muddle' and spiritual aridity, he peeps into the possibility of the 'new life' which to him is the only means to create a reintegrated life of 'man being' and 'woman-being'. D. H. Lawrence like Somerset Maugham is a 'terribly religious' artist. He rejects the wisdom of intellect and believes that the wisdom of intellect brings nothing but confusion, spiritual barrenness and human suffering at large. Lawrence condemns the concept of Utopia that promises man a higher kind of intellectual elevation but Lawrence rejects the idea of scientific evolution for he feels that the bond of blood-intimacy alone projects the true identity of man, He writes eloquently; "As for me, as for as I can, I will serve myself, for I believe that the highest virtue is to be happy, living in the greatest truth, not submitting to falsehood"[53]. D. H. Lawrence feels the World has lost the wisdom of blood-intimacy. Hence he feels man as a Hamlet without the prince of Denmark. This wiping out of blood-intimacy makes man suffer from alienation and rootlessness. To D. H. Lawrence, the 'Old world' has decayed the congenial atmosphere of international understanding. In his opinion, it is the human instinct which forms the rhythmical pattern of life. He therefore, argues to avoid undue dependence on human consciousness and 'knowing'. Lawrence ardently wants to rid the society of the old world which has brought limitless violence, horror of war, treachery and moral depravity. He loathes the 'Play-boy' attitude to life it has brought mere sensationalism, alienation and discord to society. From this aspect, he believes in the sanctity of marriage rather than mere sensationalism. 'Money-world' Lawrence thinks is one of the deadening factors of human feelings. Lawrence feels that human instinct has power enough to undo the harm the machine age has brought to man. In his letter to Lady Ottoline Morell, Lawrence writes clearly; "After the war the soul of the people will be so maimed and so injured that it is horrible to think of. And this shall be the new hope: that there be a life where in the struggle shall not be for money or for power, but for individual freedom and common effort towards good"[54]. I feel that the language needs to be freed of various artificial taboos and shut doors only make of social insanity". This shows that the instinct dominated life of perkin and constance, symbolizes the liveliness, palpable emotions and throbbing of human feelings which have vanished from the modern world. Thus D. H. Lawrence wants to reject the senile, sneaking and uncongenial 'Old world' which has caused the cessation of basic human feelings and associations. He through his novels, aspires to form a meaningful and balanced man-woman relationship. Both, D. H. Lawrence and George Orwell belong to the humanistic tradition for they argue powerfully that man should be given opportunity and freedom enough to pass a life of his own individual integrity. They never argue to succumb to the evil forces. George Orwell in his novels too rebels against falsehood, betrayal and totalitarianism of the power hungry societies. He basically believes that the dignity of man should be restored by democratic socialism and common decency. D. H. Lawrence says that man can be happy only in being part of the divine wisdom. This shows his mystical insight into the currents and cross-currents of life. George Orwell, on the one hand, pins his hope on the life of the common man, D. H. Lawrence on the other hand, feels that man's chaotic state can be re-integrated only after having a firm belief in the philosophy of 'blood intimacy'. Hence George Orwell's democratic socialism and common decency seem to be an extended metaphor of D. H. Lawrence's blood intimacy.

Maugham breaks new ground to spiritualise man's ever growing consciousness. Lawrence explores the primitive and instinctual patterns of life to dispel spiritual sterelity of the modern age. Lawrence wholeheartedly sees man's emancipation in his retrieval from the monstrosity of the mercantile world. Subjectivity is the principal driving force of inspiration in Maugham's dialectics of freedom. His dialectical art achieves universality as he makes the subjective objective. Maugham writes; "Can an artist give you more or better than himself? I shall never grow tired of asserting that it is the artist's personality, and that alone, which gives the work of art its enduring significance"[55]. Maugham however, by his dialectical art does his best to project objectivity in a work of art. He writes; "Now I am not a critic and it is not my business to criticise"[56]. 'The summing up' in which Maugham applies the principles of aesthetics, is neither "an autobiography nor it is a book of recollections"[57]. The subjective experiences while creating a work of art Maugham undergoes, become a vehicle of giving shape to his life and works. At the same time Maugham's fictional art attain's maturity as he makes the subjective objective by his dialectical art. Maugham critically writes; "I do not care if people are interested in me or not. I have no desire to impart my knowledge I have to others nor do I feel the need to correct them if they are wrong. You can get great deal of entertainment out of tedious people if you can keep your head"[58]. Maugham is critical of a typical professional writer who tends "to liberate his spirit of subject"[59]. Hence it is the liberty of fiction' which Maugham enthusiastically aspires for; "I sighed for the liberty of fiction and I thought with pleasure of the lonely reader who was willing to listen to all I had to say and with whom I could effect an intimacy that I could never hope for in the garish publicity of the theatre"[60].

Sean O' casey and Noel Coward are the two Irish contemporaries, too believed in the total transformation of the 'world' order. They speak clearly that myth and historical sense may give partial meaning to the ghastly life style but real happiness can be achieved by making the litmus turn red. William Empson exposes seven types of ambiguities. Maugham was well aware of the 'ambiguities'[61] caused by the new morality of science. James Joyce is too aware of the mundane and ethereal realities which have proneness to embroil man in seeking satisfaction on the physical and rationalistic planes. Joyce is averse to the explication of beauty which doesn't have the power of creating aesthetic emotion. Hence to Joyce, it is 'the rythm of beauty immanent in man which creates impetus to escape from the mundane experiences.'[62] Both Philip Carrey and Stephen Dedalus achieve artistic maturity in which the rhythm of beauty comes up the mundane realities of life and becomes part of the aesthetic and dialectical whole. "Rhythm, said Stephen, is the first formal esthetic relation of part to part in any esthetic whole or of an esthetic whole to its part or parts or of any part to the esthetic whole of which it is a part"[63]. Maugham therefore dialectically argues that the 'ambiguities' inculcated by the new morality of science can be removed by filling them up with the ethical, aesthetic and metaphysical vision. From the aesthetic and mystical backgrounds the novels of Somerset Maugham come up from the subjective to the objective plane. Maugham was a rebel against society, art and establishment. He was trying to establish a world order in which love was the guardian angel.

References

1. Walter Allen, The English Novel, Penguin Books, p. 326
2. Arnold Bennet; "The Old wives' tale", Hodder and Stoughton, London, New York, Toronto, p. 2.
3. *Ibid.*, p. 407.
4. *Ibid.*, p. 410.
5. John Milton, Paradise Lost (Book One), published by Rajhans Prakashan Mandir, Meerut, ed., 1981, p. 118.
6. Anthony curtis, Somerset Maugham, Weidenfield and Nicolson, London, Printed in Great Britain by Butler and Tanner Ltd., Frome, and London, p.69.
7. Quoted by Anthony Curtis, "Somerset Maugham", p. 69.
8. *Ibid.*, p. 69.
9. Brombert Victor, The novels of Flaubert: "A study of themes and techniques", Princeten, New Jeresy, Princeton University Press, ed., 1966, p. 8.
10. Atkins John, Aldous Huxley: A critical study, calder and Boyars, London, ed., 1967, p. 127.
11. *Ibid.*
12. *Ibid.*
13. Aldous Hixley; *Barve New World*, Penguin Books, ed. 1966, p. 179.
14. D. H. Lawrenesce; "The Plumed Serpent", Penguin Books, (in association with Heinemann), ed., 1979, p. 20
15. *Ibid.*, p. 80
16. D.H. Lawrence; The Lost Girl, Penguin Books, in Association with William Heinemann Ltd. ed., 1950, p. 150.
17. Leo Tolstoy; "Anna Karenina", Pan Books, in Association with William Heinemann, ed., 1977, p. 148.

18. *Ibid.*, p. 757.
19. Atkins John, p. 142.
20. *Ibid.* p. 3.
21. *Ibid.* p. 3.
22. Willam Shakespeare; King Lear, The complete works, The English Language Book Society and Collins, London, Glasgow, ed. 1964, p. 1090.
23. Quoted by Robert G. Olson; An introduction to existentialism, Dover Publications, Inc., New York, ed., 1962, p. 4.
24. Kalidasa; Sakuntala, Three Sanskrit plays, Penguin Books Ltd., Harmondsworth, Middlesex, England, ed., 1981, p. 45.
25. *Ibid.*, pp. 47-48.
26. Oscar Wilde; The picture of Dorzan Gray, p. 181.
27. *Ibid.*
28. *Ibid.*, p. 109.
29. *Ibid.*, p. 186.
30. Somerset Maugham; Great Novelists and their novels, The John C-Winston Company, Philadelphia, Toronto, ed., 1948, p. 243.
31. *Ibid.*, 245.
32. *Ibid.*
33. *Ibid.*
34. W. Somerset Maugham; The Moon and Six Pence, A Penguin international edition, Penguin Books Ltd., Harmondsworth, ed., 1970, p.6.
35. Arnold Isenberg, Aestheticism and the Theory of Criticism, the University of Chicago Press and London, ed., 1973, p. 36.
36. Ibid., p. 52.
37. Arnold Isenberg, p. 51.
38. *Ibid.*, p. 53.
39. *Ibid.*, p. 70.
40. *Ibid.*, p. 52.
41. *Ibid.*, p. 52.
42. *Ibid.*, p. 70.

43. Brombert Victor; The Novels of Flaubert: the study of themes of techniques, Princeton, New Jersy, Princeton University Press, ed., 1966, p. 5.
44. *Ibid.*, p. 5.
45. Brombert Victor, p. 66.
46. Quoted by Brombert Victor, p. 7.
47. W. Somerset Maugham Great novelists and their novels, the John C-Winston Company, Philadelphia, Toronto, ed., 1948, p. 241.
48. Quoted by Stanley Traub, Literary Criticism of Oscar Wilde, University of Nebraska Press, Lincoln, ed., 1976, p. 9.
49. Somerset Maugham; 'The partial view, William Heinemann Ltd., Melbourne, London, Toronto, ed., 1954, p. 43.
50. James Joyce, A Portrait of the artist as a young man, Penguin Books, ed., 1976, p. 8.
51. *Ibid.*, p. 247.
52. Oscar Wilde; The picture of Dorian Gray, pp. 109-110.
53. D.H. Lawrence; The Letters of D.H. Lawrence, edited by Aldous Huxley, London, William Heinemann, ed. 1932, p. 317.
54. *Ibid.*, p. 220.
55. Somerset Maugham; "Variation on a theme", The portable, Dorothy Parker, New York, the Viking Press, ed., 1962, p. 17.
56. Ibid., p. 14.
57. Somerset Maugham; The Summing up, Pocket Books ed., 1967, p. 1.
58. *Ibid.*, p. 48.
59. *Ibid.*, p. 134.
60. *Ibid.*, p. 114.
61. Quoted by George Watson, The literary Criticism, Penguin, Books, Harmondsworth, ed., 1964, p. 206.
62. James Joyce; The Portrait of the Artist as a young man, p. 206.
63. *Ibid.*

4
Ethical Imagination

The dynamics of aesthetic sensibility in Somerset Maugham's novels, explores various naunces of art and literature in all its shades and designs. The fictional art he carves out, forms a counterpoise between his ethics and aesthetics in his exploration of dialectical art, Maugham never divulges from his assertion of morality. Maugham writes; " I will continue to write moral stories in rhymed couplets. But I should be thrice a fool if I did it for aught but my own entertainment"[1]. The exquisite beauty, art, clairvoyance and the flamboyant emotions which he intermingles with his dialectical art equivocatively creates transcendence and artistic excellence. A dialectical perspective enables Maugham to project man with a larger perspicacity to aesthetically look into the intricacies of human life and define him 'self' in the mechanically estranged world. Maugham is conscious of the factors which remain at the back of his mind while logistically reasoning out human relationships in varied emerging human propositions. Maugham's yearning for a harmonious life of ethics and aesthetics with the inertia of achieving a fuller realization of human life basically gives impetus to his dialectics of freedom. Bertrand Russell explores the ethical metaphysics in order to know the Unknown. "Ethical metaphysics, says

Bertrand Russell, is a fundamentally an attempt, however disguised, to give legislative force to our own wishes. This may, of course, be questioned, but I think that it is confirmed by a consideration of the way in which ethical notions arise. Ethics is essentially a product of the gregarious instinct, that is to say, of the instinct to co-operate with those who are to form our own group against those who belong to other groups"[2]. Bertrand Russell brings into focus the conflict operating between desires and instincts. The conflict operating between desire and conflict causes human bondage. Russell rationalistically says that reason acts as a regulator of the conflict taking place between desire and passion. Russell writes; "Ethics is in origin the art of recommending to others the sacrifices required for co-operation with oneself. Hence, by reflexion, it comes, through the operation of social justice, to recommend sacrifices by oneself, but all ethics, however refined, remains more or less subjective"[3]. It can thus syllogistically be argued that the relation between truth and beauty; ethics and aesthetics implict in Maugham's delineation of dialectical art, remains at the uppermost. Limiting Somerset Maugham to be merely a Naturalistic writer, would be tantamount to limiting his fictional art. Like Shaw, Maugham never misses his moral overtones. He delves deep into the human psyche building up a rationale for probing the intricacies of human predicament. Maugham is perturbed at the way the mechanical progress of the 'Brave New World', puts obstacles to the spiritual and metaphysical dimensions of human life. Maugham with no less vigour, emphasizes the inrush of the primitive and instinctual forces which make inroads into the human consciousness and manifest them in various syllogistic propositions. Maugham is not merely a painter, a truth-seeker and a philosopher. He is a complete artist reposing his affirmation in every human endeavour man applies to ameliorate his suffering. Aesthetic beauty in Maugham's dialectical art creates in Man an urge; a palatable force to manifest itself in every human relationship he aspires for. Maugham's attitude to life, hence says Richard Aldington, is "not especially popular one of truth-seeker and truth-teller and his method as an artist is the exacting are of unadorned and uncompromising precision and clarity"[4]. Aldington disagrees with those critics who take Maugham to the merely a Naturalistic writer. Richard Aldington on the other hand points out at the 'human factor' which is inherent in Man, functions as a 'moving transport of poetry'. Aldington writes; "My own impression is that Maugham knows more about literature, philosophy and painting and has better taste than his critics"[5]. What Maugham is basically concerned is to dialectically explore every iota of human Nature taking into account how man pitted against the odds of human life, defines his 'self' in the strange and hostile world. Aldington regards Maugham as a human writer always committed to the cause of aesthetically exploring the inertia of the self with firm assertion for emancipating Man from the mere attainment of the scientific and intellectual growth of life in which Man finds himself nothing but a shadow of his former self. Aldington writes; "He is greatly gifted both as an unconscious and conscious observer of human beings; and he possesses an exact and vivid memory. Maugham is naturally a shy man, and the shy man's instinctive wish to avoid his fellow creatures could only have been broken down an even greater interest in them and passion for the art of presenting therein words"[6]. Maugham's novels are thus an incessant search for emancipating man from every form of human bondage. Exploring every form of human bondage that puts human spirit in fetters, is the principal motif behind Maugham's art and literature. Unlike Orwell Maugham does not explore the onslaught of totalitarianism and the double speak. Maugham instead, concentrates on solipsism. To him the doctrine of the self 'alone can take man to the metaphysical and mystical planes. It can thus be argued that Maugham's dialectics of freedom projects a perception for exploring manifold nuances of aesthetic sensibility. 'His novels like' 'The Moon and Six Pence', 'The Razor's Edge', 'Cakes and Ale', and 'Of Human Bondage' present Maugham's search for a world wherein he could come up the shackles of mundane world; a world of beauty, art and perfection; palatable enough to cater to the needs of aesthetic sensibility enabling him to envision freedom to be realised on the dilectical plane. The protagonists Maugham Portrays can't afford to take less than whatever they yearn for, is enough to draw a line of demarcation between the sacred and the profane. Shaw's search for emancipation is ostensibly limited to emancipating Man from the tentacles of evils prevailing in the real world. D. H. Lawrence ardently unfolds the philosophy of blood-intimacy, which to him plays a pivotal role in shaping up and synchronizing Man's identity. Maugham on the other hand solipsistically projects his novels concentrating on the inertia of the self. Unlike G. B. Shaw, Graham Greene and Evelyn Waugh, Maugham delineates the play of deep and flamboyant emotions making inroads into the intricacies of human nature. In 'Wuthering Heights', the savage passions of love create in Heathcliff a new being. Struck by the upsurge of the savage and elemental emotions, Heathcliff is embroiled at the way they inundate and corrode into his being. Heathcliff can do nothing to tame the untamed violent emotions which tear him from within. Maugham like Emily Bronte is conscious of the stark savage passions corroding deep into the being of man. Orwell escapes from emotions finding a way out in the spectre of the double speak realising that emotions existing within the being of man are themselves a larger reality. The doctrine of the innerself is thus the basis on which characters in Maugham's realm of fiction aspire for realising their world of freedom they dream of. In his dialectics of freedom, Maugham evolves a philosophy to equipoise and rationalize those untamed violent emotions which inflict man and hold him in state of bondage. Thus the dialectical approach Maugham applies, creates in man a faculty; an awareness of raciocinating the play up of the savage passions paving a way out for unfettering man from human bondage. Maugham dialectically looks to the world at large taking into account the aesthetic values which put the human soul in frenzy. From this standpoint, Maugham applies his dialectical art to differentiate between the sacred and the profane. The tragic flaw in King Lear brings him to the basics of his transactions of life. Before renouncing Cordelia, Lear is not even aware of the fury of his elemental passions thus mysteriously upturns the apple cart of his life making him subdue before them. Hence, to Maugham, the doctrine of the inner self alone can make man extirpate spiritual sickness, loneliness and alienation from the mainstream of life. Like Lawrence, Maugham too believes that the paradox of human suffering can be fathomed taking into account the basic instincts. In Maugham's fictional art, the camouflage of the sacred and the profane evokes paradox. The knowledge of inner self thus stakes and puts up piles of fire and brim stone into the mettle of characters enkindling their self with a new sense of aesthetic perception. Aristotle regards "Ethos"[7] as a moral element in the delineation of character. 'Ethos' is an expression of moral purpose where as "Dianoia"[8] is the thought, the intellectual element which projects in man the propensity to apply the rationalistic behaviour. Dianoia which delineates the intellectual element becomes an instrument through which 'ethos' finds out word expression. Maugham thus basically points out at the dynamism of the dianoia, the raison d'ètre which forms the basis of Maugham's dialectical perception of human life. It can however be said that in Maugham's dialectical system of thoughts in which 'ethos' and 'Dianoia' are made to form a mechanism of human expression.

Maugham's novels like 'The Moon and Six Pence', 'Cakes and Ale' and 'The Painted Veil' explore various areas of human bondage. The solipsistic technique Maugham applies, basically attempts at knowing the unknowableness of human nature. Lawrence on the one hand, emphasizes the philosophy of blood intimacy which makes indelible imprint on to the human psyche. Maugham on the other hand enthusiastically applies the solipsistic technique to prevent man from being split up in the modern context. Maugham is pre-empted with the anguish of exploring the aesthetic sensibility in order to present the whole picture of man. The inner knowledge man accumulates by virtue of the solipsistic power, says Maugham, compels Man to define his 'self' in the mechanically estranged world. The conflict emanating from the urge to define the 'self' and the obstacles which cause cessation of ethical growth of life—provides the turf on which man shapes up his life. Unlike Shaw Graham Greene and Waugh.

Maugham puts into the fabric of work of art the deep and turbulent emotions making them manifest into the behavioural patterns. From this aspect, Maugham's novels are evocative of the savage emotions which devilishly tear man from within. The dark and savage elemental passions annihilate Heathcliff pushing him into the labyrinth of melancholy. The arrogance inherent in Lear makes him renounce his fair daughter Cordelia, ironically sharpens the difference between the sacred and the profane. The declamatory speeches made by Lear, is indicative of how he is overwhelmed with the obnoxious and arrogant feelings of contempt. Like Swift Maugham is no misanthrope. As Maguham is dialectically conscious of both the ethical and aesthetic values, he sincerely aspires for exploring each and every iota of the being which remains manifest in Man. While exploring the manifold colours of human nature, Maugham relies on the doctorine of the innerself on the basis of which he carves out various situations man surrepticiously comes across in his search of the new avenues of freedom. In Maugham's fictional art, the camouflage of indifference, put on his characters, evokes paradoxical meaning. Unlike Maugham, V.S. Naipaul explores the riddle of the human existence. His novels like, 'The enigma of arrival' and 'A house of Mr. Biswas' are an incessant search to explore the anguish of the new settlers who look back to know and see their racial, cultural and religious roots. The endless search for identity to know the riddle of the human existence, simply makes Naipaul pre-empt with an urge to unburden the anguish of the self. Naipaul in his fictional art applies the technique of parallelism and contrast in order to see up to which degree the cultural degeneration has corroded into and unsettled them from their roots which they once belonged to. The art of caricature made at the loss of the visage of identity, enables Naipaul to explore the anguish and loneliness of the new settlers who find themselves in the alien surroundings. Naipaul keeps his eyes wide open on the present. The 'change' he sees presents fragmentary and unwholesome picture of man. As man portrayed in Naipaul's canvas of fictional art, remains alienated from the 'pastness of the past' lacking clarity of vision. Man thus projected by Naipaul, is an amalgamation of multitudes of identities into one which causes intellectual abberation. Naipaul looks at life in terms of 'the changes' that crop up into the inner cleavage of the human mind. The change and moral hierarchy brought about by the upsurge of the colossal 'change' of perception in terms of the social, cultural, political and racial consciousness, gives new twists and turns to Man's identity. Naipaul writes; "But the idea of unchanging life was wrong change was constant. People died; people grew old, people changed houses; houses come up for sale. That was one kind of change. My own presence in the valley, in the cottage of the Manner, was an aspects of another kind of change"[9]. Naipaul shows his anguish and loneliness experienced by man finding himself beset with the new surroundings, creates in him black despair. The ever growing 'change' in human consciousness from Naipaul's view results in the shuffling up and amalgamation of perspectives, outlooks and identities. Naipaul writes; "The birbed wire fence down the straight stretch of the drove- way - that also was change every one was ageing, everything was being renued or discarded"[10]. Maugham unlike Naipaul has reason, sensitiveness and imagination to 'spiritualise' and bring into fold the 'change' and hierarchy which bemuse human consciousness. Man in

Naipaul's canvas of fictional art never achieve liberation from the onslaught of ever growing change taking place on the compass of human consciousness. Man in Naipaul's world goes on to remain imprisoned and embroiled by the enigma of human existence. They go on to remain entwined and ensnared into the endless labyrinth of the search for identity and the existential problems emanating from the 'change' he perceives. The characters Naipaul creates, remain shut up into the illusiveness of the 'change' they perceive failing to establish a relation between the finite and the infinite. Unlike Maugham V.S. Naipaul gets embroiled in unentwining Man's enigma of arrival. The endless search for identity to know the riddle of the human existence, simply makes Naipaul pre-empt with a desire to unburden the agony of the 'self'. Naipaul in his fictional art, applies the technique of parallelism in order to see up to which degree the cultural degeneration has corroded man and dismantled him from his roots which he once belonged to. Maugham, on the other hand, employs the solipsistic technique and comes to believe that it is the knowledge of the self which alone can unfold the unknowableness of the 'enigma' of the human existence. Maugham, feels himself perturbed at the spiritually aberrated life. Maugham's novels are typically modern in the sense that he delves deep into the riddle of the human existence by applying the dynamics of dialectics. The ethical imagination embedded to his dialectical art explores the mystery of human relationship and exposes the paradoxical hierarchy of the externalities of human behaviour. Lear's inability to understand the paradox of suffering leads him to insanity. The inherent cruelty of the pelican daughters shows how a dialectical approach to life can bring greater Joy and fulfilment to human aspirations. The characters portrayed in Maugham's realm of fiction, are passionate and embued with the zest of defining the self while scrambling for search of 'liberation' wherein they could define the stance of their life. The characters portrayed on the mantle of his fictional art thus prisoners of their own elemental and sublime emotions, exercise great turmoil and commotion from within while scrambling for the search of freedom they make all out effort to remain true to their self. In Maugham's macrocosm of the elemental World, 'sexual instinct' plays a vital role in unfolding and defining the 'self' in the alien world. Man, says Maugham feels himself caught up and embroiled at the situations which menacingly tend to uproot his identity. The rebellion against the established order of the social milieu, operates in such a way that Strickland's wife, Ata fails to notice the change that changes his perception of the real life. Ata feels herself outsider insider after Strickland surreptiously shifts his loyalty in search of a society where he could unfold and define the self. Susie in Maugham's 'The Magician' draws up Arthur's sketch on the ontological plane. Margaret is made an object of necromancy and the way she is conjured up, symbolises how the human endeavour gets annihilated in thwarting the deep-seated evil. Loyalty in Maugham's exploration of human nature can be dealt within the implicit meaning of the instinctual pattern of life. Likewise Strickland in his search of "freedom and eternal truth"[11] goes to the extent of renunciating his family. The basic instincts implicit in him, compel him to leave England and forsake Ata, his wife. The 'sexual instinct' in Maugham's exploration of human nature embodies a creative force and hence is not a spent up force, instead it creates in man an urge to seek participation in every stance of human life. The 'sexual instinct' implicit in Maugham's characters creates in them an urge to define human relationship catering to the needs of aesthetic sensibility. Undergoing a change of heart, Strickland, goes to Paris in order to be a painter. Nothing can divulge him from inventing a life of 'liberation'. The inherent desire to live a life of 'truth and freedom' makes him wholly indifferent to the conventional ethics. Ironically Strickland remains unperturbed at the plight of suffering which surreptiously comes upon Ata. Thus, the characters like Strickland, Mrs. Drifield and Kitty never look back and bother to unburden the agony of loneliness. Liza Lambeth pathetically fails to identify the areas which could take her to the road to freedom. In a bid to come up her life of fret and fever she ironically falls prey to Jim's libido and meets with her tragic plight of loneliness. Maugham's characters are never after 'happiness'. Instead what they are after is 'pleasure'; a harmonious life of ethics and aesthetics. Like William Blake, Maugham realizes the ugliness and beauty are the two faces of the same coin. It is in this context that Maugham explores primitiveness and passion; sensuality and strangeness; duality and perfection. Maugham thus rejoices his art of ambivalence by intermingling ethics and aeshthetics. He wholeheartedly relies on the doctrine of the innerself in building up human relationships on the canvas of fictional art. His characters are neither equipped with the art of double speak nor with too much awareness of the outside World; they go on to renew their relationships on the basis of the knowledge of the innerself. For Strickland going back to his wife and the World he has forsaken, would be tantamount to putting more inflictment into his soul. Being moved up by the onslaught of the violent elemental emotions, Strickland deserts matrimony and aspires for metaphysical and spiritual dimensions of life. In order to know the unknowableness of the primitive, sublime and elemental passion, Strickland divulges from one human predicament to another in order to discover and know the realm of the truth and freedom. Thus the function of aesthetics says Somerset Maugham is to draw a line of demarcation between the good and evil; the ugly and the beautiful. All Maugham's protagonists right from the inception of their consciousness are embroiled by their aesthetic emotion.

The basic problem for Maugham's protagonists is how to define their self in a society in which money controls morality. Maugham on the ontological plane, draws a line of demarcation between 'happiness' and 'pleasure'. From Maugham's aesthetic stand point, happiness is related something with the perception the way one looks at. Maugham thus delves deep into the root cause of man's alienation and rootlessness. All the scientific and intellectual progresses made to retrieve man from the economic deprivation, exploitation and other ills of society, ultimately take man to the materialistic preponderance. The rationale behind the cropping up of the masochistic society, says Somerset Maugham, is alien to the aesthetic and metaphysical dimensions of life. In Milton's 'The Paradise Lost' the transgression of eating the forbidden fruit, embroils Adam and Eve into the throes of loneliness. Thus the 'fair' inculcated by virtue of the materialistic pursuit of life, says Maugham, ends with the 'foul'. All the materialistic progress, the glamour and glory inculcated for providing hedonistic pleasure ends up with the dissipation of individuality in the

Brave New World which pushes man to 'unhappiness' and endless labyrinth of loneliness. Maugham's characters like Strickland, Blanche, Tom and Liza yield to their inherent susceptibilities of the basic instincts. The modern novelists like Virginia Woolf, Dorothy Richardson and William Faulkner explicate human life in terms of the interior monologues making the streams of consciousness manifest in the 'Luminous Halo'. They explore the psychic processes operating into the human mind for evocating the knowledge of the innerself in the psycho-analytical terms. Blanche's aversion and hatred directed at Strickland, bears a paradoxical meaning. The agony of being repulsed and treated with contempt, raciprocally makes his being undergo a change of heart. The utter humiliation borne to him in the face of being treated with indifference, evokes in him a new meaning of the human existence. Strickland surreptiously becomes aware of his new being which for him changes the whole complexation of life. W.B. Yeats in his later poetry grapples with the problems of old age. Growing old and losing vigour and physical vitality, to Yeats, is a mocking absurdity. The older he grows the more emotionally violent he becomes. The untamed violent emotions which cease his soul up in the prime of his life, tear Strickland from within. Maugham thus dialectically argues that the violent emotions of love and its instinctual patterns of life, have a being of their own adding up new meanings of identity in the neo-mechanical society. The urge to define the self is one of the crucial factors shaping up the varied identities in the modern World. As Strickland is treated with contempt and indifference, his falling in love with Blanche, is a new revelation to Dirk. It is Blanche's repulsion that makes Strickland yield to her. Strickland says; "I don't want love. I haven't time for it. It's weakness. I am a man, and sometimes I want a woman. When I've satisfied my passion I'm ready for other things. I can't overcome my desire, but I hate it; it imprisons my spirit; I look forward to the time when I shall be free from all desire and can give myself without hindrance to my work. Because women can do nothing except love, they've given it a ridiculous importance. They want to persuade us that it's the whole of life. It's an insignificant part. I know lust. That's normal and healthy. Love is a disease. Women are the instruments of my pleasure; I have no patience with their claim to be helpmates, partners, companions"[12]. Like Larry and Philip, Strickland grapples with the earthly and the mundane love which imprisions man by making him a mere spent up force.

Beauty to Dorian Gray comes as a revelation. Strickland too has revelation of his innate instincts. Maugham loathes this play-boy attitude to life and writes; "You rejoice in your freedom, and you feel that at last you can call your soul your own."[13] I. A. Richards rightly regards the human mind as a 'System of Impulses'. Maugham and I. A. Richards in identical ways opine that experiences depend upon the play of impulses. Each new experience says I. A. Richards disturbs the impulses. The mind undergoes a state of commotion and discord unless it gets itself satisfied with those impulses creating disturbance into the substance of the human mind. Maugham in an identical way believes that the receptacle of the human mind readjusts itself with those new impulses adding new experiences. Both Lawrence and Maugham in their identical ways look into the Unknown discarding the earthly and the mundane love. In Lawrence's 'Women in love', Ursula looks for metaphysical realization of life discarding profanation of the earthly love. Realizing the metaphysical dimension of love Ursula tells Gurdun; "No", said Ursula, "It isn't. Love is too human and little. I believe in something inhuman, of which love is only a little part. I believe what we must fulfil comes out of the unknown to us, and it is something infinitely more than love. It isn't so merely human."[14] Ursula savours the earthly and the mundane experiences of love looking for a new ethics of metaphysics and spirituality in order to look into the Unknown. Discarding and abjuring his own family and everything that he owes, Strickland undergoes from one experience to another so that he might utlimately call his soul his own. Bertrand Russell places Huxley's characters in 'a physiological'[15] order. "Love, says Bertrand Russell has its own proper ideals and its own intrinsic moral standards."[16] Russell further writes; "The claims of love to a recognized place in human life are, as we have seen, very great. But love is an anarchic force which, it is left free, will not remain within any bounds set by Law and Custom."[17] Russell like Maugham delves deep into the ethical and aesthetic aspects of love which seek its own morality even in the scientific paradise. Russell writes; "Such love, like everything that is great and precious, demands its own morality, and frequently entails a sacrifice of the less to the greater, but such sacrifice must be voluntary, for, where it is not, it will destroy the very basis of the love for the sake of which it is made."[18]

In 'The Moon And Six Pence', Strickland is suddenly overtaken by a mysterious power of instincts that devastates his matrimonial life making his wife, Ata lurch in loneliness. At the same time he feels a sense of liberation and takes a sigh of relief after he breaks the bond of matrimony. Richard Aldington appreciates Maugham's passion for exploring art and beauty. In 'The Moon And Six Pence', Maugham says Richard Aldington, produces a vivid "picture of the artist who sacrifices everything for the sake of art."[19] Maugham's aesthetics has a dialectical perception and insight to appreciate humour, irony and sarcasm as well. Appreciating the art of Dorothy Parker's stories, Maugham aestheticaly writes; "Her style is easy without being slipshod and cultivated without affection. It is a perfect instrument for the display of her many-sided humour, her irony, her sarcasm, her tenderness, her pathos. Perhaps what gives her writing its peculiar tang is her gift for seeing something to laugh at the belligerent tragedies of the human animal. It is a devastating truth that she has discovered, and a salutory one, that there is something irresistibly comic in our most heartfelt woes."[20] Taking into account the ethics and aesthetics which remain interwoven into the texture of Dorothy Parker's stories Maugham appreciates her love for logic and common sense. Maugham writes; "In a few short perfect lines she presents herself to you, to take or to leave, with her pain, her laughter, her tenderness, her feeling for beauty, her ribaldry and her common sense."[21]

Maugham thus unflinchingly makes affirmation of his belief in the artist's personality which alone can work as a yardstick to dispell the maladies like rootlessness and alienation. Bergson in his elaboration of 'Elan Vital' emphasizes the artist's personality to be the principal driving force for dismantling chaos and spiritual disorganisation. D.H. Lawrence too disagrees with Eliot's concept of the extinction of personality and puts emphasis on the art of subjectvity. Agreeing with Lawrence's art of subjectvity, Maugham writes eloquently; "I ask you, can an artist give you more or better than himself? I shall never grow tired of asserting that it is the artist's personality, and that alone, which gives you the work of art its enduring significance."[22]

Maugham was influenced by great thinkers like Aristotle, Goethe, Shaw, Maupassant and Herry James. He builds up his ethical imagination on his adherence to bring into focus various iota of human nature in all his traits and characteristics. In his various essays Maugham writes that the function of art is 'not to instruct but to please'. For him the 'survival of the individual' is the greater truth that he unflinchingly rejoices in his exploration of human nature. Maugham is a keen but impartial observer of human nature. He with utmost objectively, exposes all the 'discrepancies' and hypocrisies that man puts on to camouflage his illusive life. Maugham ethically writes; "A sense of humour leads you to take pleasure in the discrepancies of human nature."[23] Maugham is neither a cynic nor a pessimist but a writer with a deep conviction to present man with all his impulse and instincts that remain implicit in him.

Maugham ethically says that art has significant role to streamline man with the ethical order. Art from Maugham's ethical stand point, can't be made to play a subservient role. He artistically writes; "For art, if it is to be reckoned as one of the great values of life, must teach man humility, tolerance,wisdom and magnanimity."[24] 'Value of Art' in Maugham's exploration of the ethical order, assumes a principal role in retrieving the society from pretension and hypocrisy. 'The value of art, says Maugham, is not beauty but right action."[25] 'The survival of the individual' hence says Maugham, can only be made possible by acting in conformity with the inertia of the self. His elaboration of ethics is not mere perfunctory; it establishes a harmonious relation between his aesthetic perception and the object he perceives in the illusive world; "The beauty of life, he says, is nothing but this, that each should act in conformity with his nature and his business"[26]. Thus, Maugham in his explication of the moral, mystical, spiritual, artistic and above all the ethical order, rationalistically argues that splitting up of personality, alienation, rootlessness and the decay of the moral order is a by product of the schism taking place between the individual and his environs. The 'survival of the individual' says Maugham can only be made possible only when man acts in conformity with his nature and business'.

In 'Catalina' Maugham, explicates the gospel of the apocalypse. He presents the picture of every woman who feels herself frenzied with the call of her inner voice which works within her as guardian angel. She fails to co-relate her mystical awareness with the external realities she is beset with. Catalina like Job seeks to know the myth of suffering which mysteriously comes upon making her bereft of her man. The 'infirmity' inculcated in her, devastatingly shatters all his dreams of attaining happiness and union in the external world. She is made to undergo limitless suffering which is mysteriously meted out to her at the hands of 'God's mills' that make her suffer immensely. Catalina cries in a melancholic strain; "why did the blessed virgin cause me to be freed from my infirmity if not that I should be fit once more to be my lover's wife ? she had pity on me and will you do nothing to help me?"[27] Maugham thus ethically argues that man has been given a limited power of vision of perceiving the persistence of illusion in the external reality. Like a Christian humanist, Maugham says Man can't know the unknowableness of the divine wisdom. As such Maugham with all his mystical insight looks into the Unknown taking man from the mundane world to the beyond. In the 'painted veil' Maugham gives ethical touch to the concept of 'beauty'. Mother Superior and her fellow sisters while working into the confines of the plague-stricken city give a 'new' meaning to their search for emancipation. Their life of renunciation and dedication to the cause of the suffering humanity; enables them to carry the white Man's burden. For them no place is alien in their understanding of Man and his environs. Beauty to Maugham devoid of ethical meaning ceases to be beautiful. Maugham hence doesn't connotate beauty merely on the literal plance. Instead Man's life steeped in aesthetic beauty can in the true sense create art and higher ideals of life. It is the ethical explication of beauty on which he draws up a line of demarcation between the ugly and beautiful. Thus, Maugham applies his dialectical art to project greater realities which could be made feasible for presenting a complete picture of human life.

References

1. W. Somerset Maugham; The Moon and Six Pence, a Penguin International Edition, Penguin Books Ltd., Harmondsworth, ed., 1979, p. 13.
2. Bertrand Russell; Mysticism and Logic, Unwin Books, London, ed., 1963, p. 82.
3. *Ibid.*
4. W. Somerset Maugham; Richard Aldington, Double Day, Doren and Co., Inc, New York, ed., 1939, p. 5.
5. *Ibid.*, p. 6.
6. *Ibid.*, p. 7.

7. W.R. Goodman; Quintessence of literacy essays, Doaba House Booksellers and Publishers, New Delhi, ed., 1980, p. 321.
8. *Ibid.*, p. 322.
9. V.S. Naipaul; The Enigma of Arrival, Penguin Books, ed., 1987, p. 34.
10. *Ibid.*
11. *Op.cit.*
12. Somerset Maugham; The Moon and Six Pence, p. 143.
13. *Ibid.*, p. 80.
14. D. H. Lawrence; Women in love, Avon publications, Inc., New York, (First edition 1920, 1922, 1948, 1958), p. 403.
15. Bertrand Russell; Marriage and Morals, Unwin Books, London ed., 1970, p. 66.
16. *Ibid.*, p. 66.
17. *Ibid.*
18. *Ibid.*, p. 158.
19. Aldington Richard, p.7.
20. Somerset Maugham, "Variation on a theme", Dorothy Parker "The Portable" (With an introduction by Somerset Maugham), New York, The Viking Press, ed., 1962, p. 15.
21. *Ibid.*, p. 18.
22. Somerset Maugham, "Variation on a theme" Dorothy Parker, The portable, pp. 17-18.
23. W. Somerset Maugham, The Summing Up, p. 49
24. *Ibid.*, p. 224
25. *Ibid.*,
26. *Ibid.*, p. 230
27. W.Somerset Maugham; Catalina, Penguin Books, ed., 1967, p. 175.

5

Labyrinth of Loneliness

Exploration of loneliness in Maugham's fictional world, is evocative of the anguish which essentially defines the self in the alien world. The cult of the materialistic and the mechanical life in retrospect makes man embroiled into the cesspool of loneliness. Man says Somerset Maugham is essentially lonely. Maugham shows profound sympathy for those who get entwined into the cesspool of loneliness. The basic driving force behind E. M. Forster's emphasis on the cultural harmony is his awareness of the self which plays a crucial role in shaping up the racial, cultural and religious identity of Man. Forster is thus conscious of the milieu which makes inroads into the human psyche and enables him to pinpoint the factors impeding the growth of human relationships. Forster thus emphasizes the need to take into account the various components of identity shaping up the being of Man. Maugham in an identical way probes the basic factors leading to the loneliness of Man. He opines that Man's proclivity to get divulged from the aesthetic sensibility, is one of the factors which give rise to loneliness. In V. S. Naipaul's novel, 'The Enigma of Arrival', the act of knowing operates at the intellectual and psychic planes. Naipaul too much relies on the yardstick of intellect. While looking back with frenzy to know where his roots lay, all the ventures undertaken to search for identity, go on to remain a mere 'enigma'. 'The Return of the Native' is thus replete with doubt, enquiry and dilemma. All the human endeavour applied by man in Naipaul's realm of freedom, are never materialised into a sense of belonging. Eliot and Yeats snigger at the abnormal growth of the human mind. As the ' 'Wastelanders' are aesthetically dried up, they have no propensity to apply the innate aesthetic sensibility for searching for the domain of 'truth and freedom'. Human life as depicted in Eliot's poetry is spiritually chaotic; a spiritually disorganised mass of 'broken images' caught up and entwined into the illusive world of 'prickly pears'. For Maugham solipcism, the doctrine of the inner self is the basic yardstick through which his characters make assertion of their inner being. Maugham's characters never undergo the dilemma of 'to be' or 'not to be'. Instead they get frenzied to create a better world at par with the wisdom of the 'self'—is the basis on which they give the stance of life. They get satisfaction and reveal in every iota of their self. Maugham's characters jostle with the frenzy of the stark passion. Maugham thus dialectically probes the rationale of attaining happiness in the modern world in which he brings into harmony the colossal growth of science and religion. Like Spinoza, Maugham existentially wants to cohere science in religion in the proper perspective. No sooner do the protagonists in Maugham's fictional art become conscious of the change of heart that subjectively shape up and make upside down the whole being of Man than they evocatively define their renewed being. The rationlistic behaviour thus enables them to see the real world with the dialectical vision. This cumulative vision of their frenzied state thus sharpens and forms their aesthetic vision. Maugham's characters thus long for limitless satisfaction they aspire for. Freedom says Somerset Maugham basically emanates from Man's innate aesthetic aspiration to define his 'self'. The realm of 'truth and freedom' for which Maugham's characters aspire, isn't supposed to be identified with the cropping up of the brave new world in which man remains indifferent to the aesthetic beauty. 'Primeval beauty' says Maugham casts esoteric and metaphysical spell upon the being of man enkindling an urge to look into the Unknown. Aesthetic beauty says Somerset Maugham should not be kept confined to the mere paraphernalia of arts for arts sake. The influx of the humanistic, primitive and the sublime above all aesthetic emotions play a significant role in presenting a complete and real picture of man in the modern world. Maugham who was equally influenced by both the Greek masters, Plato and Aristotle. Plato on the one hand opines that the worth of poetry should be evaluated by "the truth of life achieved by the imitation, not by the pleasure it gives."[1] Maugham agrees with Plato that the object imitated must be 'beautiful'. Being a critic of the varied naunces of art, Maugham strikes a balance between the dictum drawn up by Plato and Aristotle. For Maugham, pleasure and beauty are inseparably associated with each other. Eliot in an identical way, criticises the contemporary critics for taking enjoyment and understanding to be distinct literary activities. Elaborating the concept of the frontiers of criticism, Eliot opines that 'understanding' and 'enjoyment' go hand in hand. Hence 'understanding' and 'enjoyment' says Eliot shouldn't be regarded as distinct literary activities instead says he should be regarded as wholesome in their applicability to the mechanics of a work of art. Maugham like Eliot gathers the impression that 'pleasure' and 'beauty' are the two inseparable integrals of a work of art. What is striking is that beauty which is manifold in Maugham's dialectical art, has both ethical and spiritual dimension. Maugham's connotation of beauty doesn't exist merely on the literal plane. Instead the implicit and multifoliate applicability of beauty remain operative on the ethical, aesthetic, spiritual and mystical planes enabling Maugham to artistically achieve empathy and clairvoyance.

The exploration of loneliness in Maugham's fictional art, is two fold. Maugham's characters remain embued with the desire of getting emancipation from the anguish they suffer from. In order to come out of the orgy of the aesthetic emotion they evoke a sense of liberation. Strickland loves living in solitude in order to know the inscrutable 'Nirvana'. Maugham's characters in spite of facing obstacles to the building up of the growth of harmonious human relationships, conflagrate with the desire to get emancipated from the trauma of loneliness. The feeling of anguish, for creating a world of their own makes them entwined and caught up in a state of hman bondage. Like Shakespeare, Maugham is aware of the 'foul' hidden in the garb of the 'fair'-Maugham thus paradoxically removes the painted veil of the coloured emotions and explores human life in terms of solipsism. Eliot symbolically reveals the sordidness of the skull whereas John Webster explicate the paradox of evil in his Jacobean play, 'The White Devil'. 'How long have I beheld the devil in crystal'. This is how Webster exposes the problem of evil which remains deep-seated and camouflaged from within. Strickland on the other hand abjures Ata and looks beyond the mundane world for carving a way out to catering to the hidden aura of elemental passions. The loneliness which lies deep-seated in 'the painted veil', is two fold making Man-Woman relationship pathetically irreconcilable. Kitty is traumatised not only at her husband's apathy, she is equally made a subject to betrayal and triviality at the hands of Townsend. She searches for her roots both in the conventional ethics and experience. She undergoes a dilemma and finds her soul ceased up with the desire of attaining emancipation from every form of bondage. A sudden revelation just emerges within her making her essentially conscious of the aesthetic power; the propensity of achieving transcendence and spiritual elevation to her life. Larry who is lacerated by the outward glamour of the cult of Americanism, no more aspires for the way of the world. All those whosoever aspire for seeking emancipation from the success-oriented life, remain ensnared into the tentacles of human bondage. Man in Maugham's world thus gets respite in getting detached from the happiness principles. In Milton's 'The Paradise Lost', Adam and Eve move up clock-wise. They commit transgression in the happy fields of the heaven and enter into the life of experience whereas in Maugham's dialectics of freedom, characters rather move up in the anticlockwise in order to make the finite a vehicle of entering the infinite. In Milton's 'The Pradise Lost', characters move up from innocence to experience but in Maugham's exploration of loneliness man gets spiritually purged only after passing through the ordeal of experience. Their frantic search for freedom takes them to the world of tanscendence where the cult of attaining happiness at the dialectical plane no more stifles and subdues the self.

Somerset Maugham's characters do not identify their self with the mainstream of the existing milieu and feel themselves stranger to the main stream of society. Strickland who abjures his domesticity aesthetically searches for new avenues of freedom. He resorts to leaving his "birth place"[2] to explore new horizons of freedom in the image of the 'self' he has within. Likewise the characters like Larry, Strickland and kitty remain hellbent upon making assertion of their identity undergoing intense anguish, turmoil and disquetitude at their inability to strike a balance between the 'self and the 'real' world; they find themselves strangers in the real world in search of their make-believe freedom and self-fulfilment. They rebel against the mainstream of the existing society in which they remain wrapped up in. Their estrangement to the existing order knows no bound as they ironically get baffled at the unknowableness of the collective psyche. Maugham solipsistically writes; "They are strangers in their birthplace, and the leafy lanes they have known from childhood or the populous streets in which they have played, remain but a place of passage. They may spend their whole lives aliens among their kindred and remain aloof among the only scenes they have ever known"[3]. Their need to come out of the tentacles of human bondage is inexorable and sacrosanct with their aesthetic aspirations. The atavistic frenzy with which they move out frantically to translate the dream of freedom into a concrete reality, shows how they are conscious of their self. The dialectics of freedom, hence says Maugham, can be realised by applying the empirical and rationalistic approach to life in order to spiritualize the senses. Maugham is deeply aware of the colossal growth of intellect. The basic problem before Maugham was how to spiritualize the colossal growth of science and intellect. To Spinoza God exists both in science and religion. Maugham like Spinoza carves out meaning, design, symphony and pattern in the facade of science and religion. The conflict operating within the substance of the human mind, is thus the root cause of the real paradox of alienation, rootlessness and spiritual crisis. Maugham's depiction of the aesthetic and metaphysical vision, opens up a new space to project the new man in the modern world. Hence understanding man with all his exigencies of life, to come out of the cocoon of bondage, projects Maugham as a post modern litterateur.

Maugham aesthetically explores human nature to the best of his knowledge. Tragedy to Somerset Maugham is neither imitation of human action nor of life, instead, tragedy lies in man's indifference to the aesthetic sensibility. It can however be dialectically argued that the problem of loneliness crops up in Man's life on account of his inability to find a co-relation between matter and spirit. Tragic flaw, in Maugham's protagonists remain hidden in their proclivity to yield to the stark savage passions. Their escape to the primitive, elemental and instinctual patterns of life acts as cathartic and cleansing effect upon them. Larry who walks tiptoe on to the 'Razor's edge', to escape from the onslaught of the materialistic and hedonistic pursuit of life in which happiness plays the pivotal role, no more feels his heart throb for entering the bond of matrimony. The horror and devastation writ large during the inclemence of war, make him decline from marrying Isabel. Kitty's accompaniment with Mother superior enables her to behold beauty writ at large in the visible.

The characters of Somerset Maugham are talkative and frank. They enthusiastically scramble for a life of emancipation from the life of bondage. The characters projected on Maugham's dialectical canvas, thrive on the evocativeness of the aesthetic sensibility which determines the shape of human relationships. Their escape to the world of imagination, primitiveness; fancy and delight, is momentary. But ironically they find themselves embroiled with the mundane realities of life in the midst. In Maugham's dialectics of freedom, Man frantically searches for various ways and means to thwart the inclemence of suffering and bondage. Eugene Marchbanks in Shaw's 'Candida' feels himself entwined into the trammels of agony. His aesthetic sensibility receives severe jerks and jolts after he finds Candida yoked in the menial work. To the horror of Eugene Marchbanks, Candida is made to grub the floor and dabble her fingers in filling the lamp with paraffin oil—shakes up all his romantic sensibility. Maugham like Shaw dialectically challenges the established code of morality. What is ironical in Shaw is that he makes emotions subdued to reason whereas Maugham elaborating the dialectics of freedom applies the rationalistic approach to human life arguing that the elemental and the primitive passions have a being of their own. Maugham dialectically argues that it would be unbecoming of Man to be unconscious of the palatable and potent fury of passions which remain deep-seated in him. Maugham thus applies his dialectical approach to probe and see how man can untrammel himself from the stark and savage passions. Philip while undergoing utter humiliation experiences the fury of the instinctive, primitive and aesthetic emotion and feels himself helpless before them. Philip-Mildred relationship thus opens up new horizons for emanating from bondage. The more Philip gets ubiquitous to Mildred the more is the degree of annihilation which pushes him to the servility of those dark savage passions. Maugham dialectically says that an ideal Man-women relationship can be made only if man discovers his self at length. It is the knowledge of the self says Maugham which alone can bring man back to the normal mainstream of life. Mildred like Liza doesn't understand the spiritual and metaphysical dimensions of love which make Philip rebel against the conventional ethics. The woman in Mildred makes his soul ceased up with the aesthetic emotion. Unlike Maugham, Shaw regards woman as a liberator from the inclemence of human suffering and loneliness. Falling prey to susceptibilities of passion, says Maugham, causes the real crux of human bondage. Woman from Shaw's concept of freedom, has been regarded as a source of creating a better race. It is Ann who persuades Tanner from building up a harmonious relationship. The image of woman, hence, in the Shavian philosophy, becomes a vehicle of generating life-force. In Maugham's 'Of Human Bondage,' it is Philip who persuades Mildred to come round his aesthetic and metaphysical perception. Passing through the drudgery of life, he becomes one among the 'down and out' and feels his throbing self from within. Philip's loneliness emanates from Mildred's inability to aesthetically communicate to him. Freedom thus to Philip is remote and distant. Maugham is a rationalistic writer in the sense that he finds the modern generation devoid of the faculty of knowing the self. As the modern generation is spiritually sick, man gets bemused at the growing intellect in the modern age. Both Eliot and Yeats lament at man's alienation from the mainstream of life. From Maugham's dialectical perspective it is the schism between the aesthetic beauty and Man's falling prey to hedonistic life, causes loneliness and alienation. Man then no more has the idea of the beautiful to perceive the aesthetic, metaphysical and mystical experiences. Maugham thus opines that it is the dynamics of the aesthetic beauty which alone can bring man back to the metaphysical and mystical ways of life. Maugham writes; "I confess that when first I made acquaintance with Charles Strickland, I never for a moment discerned that there was in him anything out of the ordinary"[4]. 'Sexual instinct' hidden in the labyrinth of human nature, creates in man a desire for discovering the world of 'truth and freedom'. Strickland never bothers for the way the real world menacingly tends to uproot his self. As such getting oblivious of the suffering which comes upon his family, he escapes to the forlorn of Tahiti in order to become a painter. He wanders about solitude and tranquility in order to know and discover the domain of the truth and freedom. Strickland's falling in love with Drove Dirk's wife, Blanche is part of the sexual instinct which shows how he instinctually urges to look into the elemental and primitive and above all into the Unknown. It is Blanche's repulsion against him which surreptitiously makes him attract to her. Strickland says; "She couldn't bear the sight of me. It amused me"[5]. The zest to know the mystery of the elemental passions, he passes from one experience to another. Thus the search for freedom taking place on the psychic, intellectual and aesthetic plane is an on going process. Maugham who is adept in the art of delving deep into the sublime and elemental emotions, is "more concerned to know than to judge"[6]. The unfolding of the labyrinth of the truth and freedom, says Somerset Maugham in unknowable. The concept of love as elaborated by Maugham, is alien to that of the real world. Love from Maugham's dialectical perspective, enkindles in man transcendence and liberation from the fret and fever of the modern world. Strickland who rebels againt the hypocrysies and pretensions of society, shows his aversion to hedonistic life. He seeks solace in the doctrine of the inner self drawing up a line between the solipsistic and the 'real' world. The confused picture of the real world holds no relevance for Strickland. Thus a dialectical relation between 'the fact and the solipsistic world' alone can brace up the matter with spirit harmoniously. Strickland says; "Facts were nothing to him, for beneath the mass of irrelevant incidents he looked for something significant to himself. It was as though he had become aware of the soul of the universe and were compelled to express it. Though these pictures confused and puzzled me. I could not be unmoved by the emotion that was patent in them; and, I knew not why, I felt in myself a feeling that with regard to Strickland was the last I had ever expected to experience. I felt an overwhelming compassion"[7]. Maugham's dialectical art thus unfolds the paradox of life on the ontological plane. His treatment of characters is paradoxical in the sense that camouflage of experience, conceals "a better secret"[8] deceiving the outside world. Blanche's hatred for Strickland paradoxically has an inkling of love for him that brings 'deliverance'. The 'Nirvana' Strickland craves for by accumulation of knowledge brings him the illusion of reaping utmost satisfaction. To Srickland women are more contemplative in nature while bringing man down to their perception of life. Behind the painted veil of hatred and ridicule there lay the deep seated love for Strickland. Blanche who is well conscious of her 'self' knows that she would not endure the vulnerability of her passions if Dirk Strove brings Strickland home. The intensity of loneliness gets further enhanced when man paradoxically fails to know the psyche of the outside world. Maugham's protagonists as such rebel against the mainstream of the conventional ethics. Philips rebels against the conventional morality and yearns for living at par with aesthetic emotion. In order to emancipate himself from the onslaught of happiness Philip passes from one ordeal to another resorting to do 'nothing'. Rebelling against the confines of Blackstable, years for knowing the conundrum of life and aesthetically caters to the needs of the 'soul'. Strickland too leaves his wife, Ata, and goes from one experience to another giving vent to the anxiety and agony of his throbbing self. As such breaking the barriers of the conventional morality, Maugham's characters temporarily get respite from the pain and loneliness and scramble for liberation. Strickland passes a secluded life in order to 'know' and unfold the inscrutable "Nirvana". Thus the anguish to come out of the trammels of infinite suffering is the basic crux on which Strickland quest for truth and freedom rests. Strickland says; "I do not know at what inscrutable Nirvana you aim. Do you know yourself? Perhaps it is Truth and Freedom that you seek, and for a moment you thought that you might find release in Love. I think your tired soul sought rest in a woman's arms, and when you found no rest there you hated her. You had no pity for her, because you have no pity for yourself. And you killed her out of fear, because you trembled still at the danger you had barely escaped"[9].

The agony of loneliness says Somerset Maugham, gets further enhanced when man paradoxically fails to 'know' the psyche of the outside world. The agony of being 'lonely' becomes tragically more intense in the face of man's inability to 'know' and convey his trauma of loneliness to the outside world. Maugham's protagonists revolt against the mainstream of the conventional society. Philip revolts against the conventional morality and yearns for living a life of aesthetic beauty. Philip passes from one experience to another rebelling against the confines of Blackstable. He yearns for knowing the conundrum of life aesthetically which caters to the needs of the soul. Likewise Strickland leaves his wife and goes from blue to the bolt to give vent to the anxiety and agony of the self. Breaking the barriers of the conventional morality, they temporarily get respite from the agony of the soul and aspires for 'liberation'. Strickland passes a secluded life in order to 'know' the 'inscrutable Nirvana' the anguish to come out of the trammels of the infinite suffering is the basic crux on which Strickland's search for 'truth and freedom' rests. The narrator tells Strickland; 'I' do not know what infinite yearning possesses you, so that you are driven to a perilous, lonely search for some goal where you expect to find a final release from the spirit that torments you. I see you as the eternal pilgrim to some shrine that perhaps does not exist. I do not know at what inscrutable Nirvana you aim. Do you know yourself? Perhaps it is Truth and Freedom that you seek, and for a moment you thought that you might find release in Love. I think your tired soul sought rest in a woman's arms, and when you found no rest there you hated her. You had no pity for her, because you have no pity for yourself. And you killed her out of fear, because you trembled still at the danger you had barely escaped.'[10] It is this urge to define the self to the world at large makes them rebel and escape to 'the far from the madding crowd' which could cater to their inner being. Living into the confines of Tahiti, Strickland remains indifferent to outside world. Attaining refinement and transcendence, to him is no less than a pilgrimage which brings freedom to his self. To the outside world, Strickland is always at variance, reticent and uncommunicative; "To these people, native and European, he was a queer fish, but they were used to queer fish, and they took him for granted; the world was full of odd persons, who did odd things; and perhaps they knew that a man is not what he wants to be, but what he must be."[11] From the existential point of view, the mystery of suffering lies in man's longing for the rational and materialistic desires. Applying the dialectical approach to man's alienation Maugham says that the reason of man's anguish and spiritual restlessness is that man wants 'to be'.[12] It is the 'nostalgia' to define the self and to unentwine himself from the tentacles of hedonestic life which creates in him the 'Unconquerable Spirit of Man'.[13] This dialectical approach to life enables Maugham's characters to create beauty, comeliness and above all freedom from the life of human bondage. Maugham comes to realise that it is aesthetic beauty which alone can take man to the truth. To Maugham aesthetic beauty creates the real threshold of man's freedom. Maugham says that aesthetic beauty is an instrument through which man savours the truth. Thus aesthetic beauty, says Maugham, opens up the floodgates of spiritual manifestation where the body and soul exists in complete unison. Maugham writes; "The artist, painter, a musician, by his decoration, sublime or beautiful, satisfies the aesthetic sense; but that is akin to the sexual instinct, and shares its barbarity: he lays before you also the greater gift of himself"[14]. D. H. Lawrence hates the hollowness of the hedonistic society which makes life stale and frigid. In Eliot's Poem, 'The

Wasteland' the applicability of'inquision' and biblical beauty has been projected on the metaphysical plane. To an agnostic it might emerge itself as 'inquisition' where as semblance might become 'a thing of beauty' to a believer. To John Keats, truth and beauty are interelated with each other but in Maugham's realm of freedom, the aesthetic beauty alone can unfold the mystery of the truth and the absolute. Maugham explicates the mystry of human life on the dialectical plane and presents the duality of experence; beauty and inquisition; good and evil; hatred and love; innocence and experience. Thus Maugham's dialectical art projects the contrast between primitiveness and modernity. In Maugham's dialectics of freedom, the attainment of 'knowledge' awakens in man the faculty of reasoning and empiricism through which man can free himself from the onslaught of the elemental, sublime and instinctual patterns as to Maugham explicates the mystery of life 'to the best of knowledge' in order to probe the enigma of the human existence. Both Maugham and Shaw regard matrimony as a serious transaction of life. The problem of loneliness achieves a different dimension, says Maugham while man in his search of freedom from the mundane society, is ensnared by the semblance of happiness. Hence to Somerset Maugham, the 'painted veil' of the real world does not constitute the real self instead, the aesthetic emotion gets manifest making the invisible visible.

In Maugham's another novel, "The Painted Veil", the agony of loneliness finds expression in the racially hostile colonial society. Kitty's lack-lustre marriage to Walter, is dovoid of the idea of the 'beautiful', gives her no freedom from the shackles of the mundane world. Even after being yoked in her matrimony, the search for freedom goes on to mesmerise her. The sudden realisation of being ensconced into the tentacles of bondage, creates in her 'a new world'[15] which she thinks is powerful enough to emancipate her from the state of bondage. Being taken to a strange colonial society, the agony of loneliness makes her filled up with anxiety. As she is made to live in the alien surroundings, matrimony to her is no longer a source of aesthetic pleasure. Maugham like Eliot laments at the jarring notes of alienation and rootlessness persisting in the mordern age. In her bid to come out of the anguish of her lack-lustre marriage, she gets entwined into another vortex of suffering and falls prey to Charlie's Libido. Maugham at the same time projects the theme of the exploiter and the exploited in the racially hostile world of the painted 'veil'. Behind this 'painted veil' of racial discrimination he treats her as a plaything; an object of desire. She grows conscious of the triviality of her relationship with Charles. The 'new' aesthetically awakened woman in Kitty, passess through the pain of loneliness, making her essentially a misfit. Walter's death in the plague-stricken city multiplies the intensity of her loneliness. Her aspiration to come out of the ennui she passes through, makes her learn the high ideals of love; self-denial hospitality and philanthropy. Kitty says to sister Joseph; "Don't you know that I'm a human being, unhappy and alone, and I want comfort and sympathy and encouragement; oh, can't you turn a minute away from God and give me a little compassion; not the christian compassion that you have for all suffering things, but just human compassion for me?".[16] This shows how Maugham raises his voice against the austerity of the conventional ethics. The device of flight employed in Maugham's 'The painted veil' enables his characters to escape from the life of fret and fever. As

Kitty feels herself caught up into the cesspool of loneliness, she aesthetically ponders to evolve a way out to live up to the expectation of her spirit; "She had thought herself free from lust and vile passions, free to live the clean and healthy life of the spirit;"[17] Kitty comes to realize a vision of freedom from bondage, suffering and guilt; a vision that could bring her back from the mundane to the transcendental plane. In order to translate her dream of freedom into a concrete, reality, she goes to the extent of resorting to 'flight'. Like Sophia Banes, she yearns for regaining her 'paradise lost' by retrograding to her house of 'provinciality' wherein she is no more a slave to her servile emotions and basic instincts; "It was neat and clean. Everything was in its place, ready for her use, but although the day was warm and sunny there was about the silent rooms a chill and desolate air."[18] The sacrifice given by Walter in the plague ridden city gives her the real meaning of freedom. She comes to realise that it is the 'self control' that could be made instrumental in retrieving the society from bondage, guilt and obsession. Kitty contemplates that "she would not admit that his death was a relief to her, she could say honestly that if by a word of hers she could bring him back to life she would say it, but she could not resist the feeling that his death made her way to some extent a trifle easier."[19] Kitty learns wisdom through suffering. The experiences and the phantasmagoria she undergoes while living in the ealier surroundings, becomes the stepping stone of her spiritual realisation. It is Mother Superior who unfolds the mystery of freedom and says that it is 'love' and 'duty' which can open the flood gates of freedom. Kitty comes to realise that emancipation from every form of bondage can be carved only when love and duty become one. Her feelings of anguish at her inability to rationalise the dark and elemental passions go enhanced when she looks back how despicably she had acted by violating the aesthetic and metaphysical manifestation of life. The ignominy of being carried away by her stark savage passion, holds herself 'in a state of bondage'. Looking back in anger and remorse she calls up how despicably falling prey to her passions, she feels her 'self' subdued and stifled. She makes confession of her vulnerability which so much heightens the pitch of her loneliness she says pathetically; "Oh, I don't blame you, I was just as bad. I yielded to you because I wanted you. But it wasn't the real me. I'm not that hateful, beastly, lustful woman. I disown her. It wasn't me that lay on that bed panting for you when my husband was hardly cold in his grave and your wife had been so kind to me, so indescribably kind. It was only the animal in me, dark and fearful like an evil spirit, and I disown, and hate, and despise it. And ever since, when I've thought of it, my gorge rises and I feel that I must vomit."[20]

Maugham thus recuperates with a renewed energy with a view to cultivating hope and reconciliation. He was well aware of the human depravity prevailing in the post-colonial society. E. M. Foster reposes his faith in the art of subjectivity by celebrating the philosophy of personal relationship. Foster, unlike Naipaul, is not worried at the hundred mutinies of the clash-culture, instead optimistically pins his hope in the building up of personal relationship. M. K. Gandhi's concept of freedom is based upon the truth. To M. K. Gandhi, it is the truth which alone can take man to the golden millennium of freedom. Truth to Gandhi is the yardstick of attainment of freedom. For Gandhi truth is beauty: palatable enough to translate the cherished dreams of freedom into reality. Maugham on the other hand says that aesthetic beauty becomes the stepping stone of freedom. Maugham is a rationalistic writer. He dialectically probes the basic reason of man's alienation and rootlessness. He dialectically believes that the inanity of the aesthetic and spiritual principles of love—is the real crux of spiritual emptiness persisting in the modern age. Maugham hence aesthetically believes that it is the dialectical approach to life which alone can bridge up the ever growing intellect with aesthetics which in turn takes man to the road to self-fulfilment and freedom. The dichotomy of the matter and spirit, says Somerset Maugham, is thus an indirect outcome of the lack of the applicability of the aesthetic principles of love.

Maugham's 'Cakes and Ale' aesthetically brings to light the conflict taking place between literature and society. As Maugham is essentially a rebel, he brings into focus those social constraints that impede the growth of the artist in the alien surroundings. In Lawrence's 'Sons and Lovers', Paul feels himself an insider outsider and applies his aesthetic sensibility in order to give vent to his poetic creativity and meaningful relationship. Stephen Dedalus, in James Joyce's 'The Portrait of an Artist as a young man' undergoes extreime pain and anguish in defining his self in the real world. Finding himself in the alien surroundings, he utilizes his humanistic and artistic powers to create a world of his own. The images of flow and the images of flight, then become a vehicle of giving a new dimension to the consciousness of his self which plays a greater role in getting himself emancipated from the mundane experiences of adolescence, guilt and obsession. The quest for greater realm of freedom, in the novels of Somerset Maugham, is the basic impetus with which his characters strive for freedom. What needs to be emphasized is that Maugham in 'Cakes and Ale', employs the first person narration to bring into focus the pretensions, oddities and hypocrisy of the real world which divide the society between 'they' and 'us'. Marx and Engels socialistically categorise the society between 'haves' and 'havenots' in which the aesthetic, spiritual and metaphysical dimensions of life have no inkling to look into the Unknown. Thus the conflict operating between man and society to rescue man from preponderance of the feudal structure, remains confined to the mere bridging up of the 'haves' and 'havenots' in which the aesthetic realizations of have no role to play. Maugham on the other hand, finds the aesthetic aspects of life humane enough to sustain man with all his quest for greater realisation in the mundane world. The characters portrayed on Maugham's dialectical canvas, know hypocrisy and camouflage. Rosie in Maugham's 'Cakes and Ale', is a character not to be seen only from the Naturalistic aspects; she embodies within no act of concealment and hypocrisy. Maugham like Shakespeare has sympathetic insight into the delineation of human nature. It is in this context in which man's proneness to obsession, guilt and triviality needs to be seen not merely from the Naturalistic perspective but also from the dialectical perspective in which the basic instincts are made intermingled with intellect. "proper study of mankind is man"[21] says Somerset Maugham scaffolding his ethical imagination. His concept of art thus essentially has ethical and moral preponderance. He was intensely conscious of the hollowness and pretence of the people living in the "real life". Maugham writes; "For if the proper study of mankind is man it is evidently more sensible to occupy yourself with the coherent, substantial, and significant creatures of fiction than with the irrational and shadowy figures of real life".[22] Maugham's characters are hence unchangeable. They are Jonsonian characters in a sense that they neither undergo a change of heart nor metamorphose into the being of otherness; they love to stay what they are from within. Rosie while living a life of seclusion intends to stay the way she would like to. Rosie says; 'No'. She smiled. "Not that I haven't had offers. I'm quite happy as I am".[23] Maugham thus assuming the voice of Ashenden, in 'Cakes and Ale', makes the subjective objective. While sharing his opinion with Mrs Driffield about the humaneness Rosie retains within her, Maugham writes; "You don't understand, I said', 'She was a very simple woman. Her instincts were healthy and ingenuous. She loved to make people happy. She loved love.

'Do you call that love?'

'Well, then, the act of love. She was naturally affectionate. When she liked anyone it was quite natural for her to go to bed with him. She never thought twice about it. It was not vice; it wasn't lasciviousness; it was her nature. She gave herself as naturally as the sun gives heat or the flowers their perfume. It was a pleasure to her and she liked to give pleasure to others. It had no effect on her character; she remained sincere, unspoiled, and artless."[24]

As Maugham is essentially a rebel, he raises his voice against the cessation of the ethical values. The artist in Maugham is baffled at the pretension and hypocrisy of the conventional society. He aesthetically intends to dismantle the feeling of otherness. Robert Frost feels himself caught up in a dilemma—like situation. The duality and ambivalence Frost creates in his poetry, disassociate the poetic sensibility. Frost's poem, 'Mending wall' evokes the voice of duality. 'We don't need the wall', says Robert Frost but in the same vein, he says; 'Good fences make good neighbours'. Frost fails to strike a balance between the discordant voice of the 'self'. He remains inconclusive as the discordant voice of the 'self' echoes repeatedly. Maugham, in an identical way too finds the pretensions of the spiritually hollow 'real life'.[25] The concept of emancipation and loneliness as analyzed by Marx and Engels, remains inconclusive and limited to the mere bridging up of the 'haves' and 'havenots' Maugham instead, applies the dialectical art to bridge up the gap between the 'haves' and 'havenots'; high and low; rich and poor and above all the Black and White. Maugham dialectically strips the persistence of pretension and hollowness of the people dwelling in the 'real' life. He says, "I do not know that the people I lived among were pretensious in the sense of making themselves out to be richer or grander than they really were, but looking back it does seem to me that they lived a life full of pretences. They dwelt behind a mask of respectability."[26] Maugham is aghast at the man-made rich-poor divisions which keep the larger humanity incommunicative.

Such categorization of 'us' and 'they' says Maugham heightens the pitch of loneliness on the 'real' plane. Maugham in 'Cakes and Ale' brings into focus the pretensions of the 'real' society, which to him is spiritually 'hollow' and discordant. Maugham writes; "We thought London people vulgar. We said it was horrid to have all that rag-tag and bobtail down from town every year, but of course it was all right for the tradespeople. Even they, however, gave a faint sigh of relief when September came to an end and Blackstable sank back into its usual peace."[27] The act of triviality lies in his mere communicating to Edward Driffield, intensifies his estrangement to the conventional society he lives in. Maugham writes; "They're most disreputable people', said my uncle. 'I don't wish you to associate with them'."[28]

Maugham's exploration of loneliness lies in Man's Proneness to consumation of love. He is aesthetically conscious that love sought in terms of consumation embroils Man in the endless annals of loneliness. The humanistic urges of seeking satisfaction in consumation of love is devoid of the aesthetics of 'association'. In Maugham's exploration of human bondage, Love is thus a sickly 'disease' which subjugates emotions. In 'The 'Moon and Six Pence', Strickland is bewildered at his sudden revolution how his proneness to seeking satisfaction on the physical plane, enchances the pitch of loneliness. The larger is the degree of his proneness to yielding to impulse, the larger is the degree of his loneliness and emotional vaccuity that alienate him from the mainstream of life. Maugham's characters thus do not conform to the conventional ethics. The life of experience they undergo itself opens up a dialectical consciousness to get retrieved from the anguish of being lonely.

Maugham had a little faith in Man's altruistic means of emancipating society from suffering and human bondage. He is dialectically conscious that the altruistic efforts applied to emancipate Man from the life of bondage ends not with 'a bang but with a whimper'. Maugham looks beyond Man's deriving satisfaction out of consumation of love. He is an aesthetic visionary who believes in the consciousness and the inertia of the 'self', one who is unaware of one's own 'self'; says Maugham, is not conscious of the greater reality hidden in the cloister of the self. Nor does he repose his faith in the psycho-analytical devices to bring into focus the inner recesses of the substance of the human psyche. In 'The Moon and the Six Pence' he comes to realize how Man's Proclivity to seek satisfaction goes on to excite his passions embroiling him in irretrievable knots of loneliness. In order to know of the fury of the sublime passion and despair, Strickland forsakes home, family and reputation. He escapes to the forlorns of and Tahiti to know how the stark and savage passions subjugate Man to a life of alienation. Julia is too disillusioned with the way she is made to make money, pelf and power; and popularity. Her sole realization that the theatrical establishments in which she is yoked with 'violence' creates in her an 'area' of 'association' . Her anguish is to free herself, from the irretrievable knots of bondage, sharpens the pain of loneliness. The theatrical establishments no more give relief to her 'senses'. In 'The Razor's Edge' the meaning of loneliness has been connotated in terms of the mystical realizations of human existence. Larry is 'lonely' enough to do 'nothing'. Both Philip and Larry are aesthetically conscious that bondage to impulse condescends Man from within. Philip's indifference to the life of Americanism and the fun and frolics is indicative of the basic fact how he declines to serve in which he no longer believes. For both Philip and Larry, putting up with the pain of loneliness is better than yielding to the cult of hedonistic aspects of life. In 'the painted veil' the meaning of loneliness has been connotated on the racial plane.

Loneliness in Eliot's poetry has different connotations. Man in Eliot's realm of poetry has been shown running after the illusive life. The centuries long evolutionary processes have turned London into 'unreal' city. Eliot laments at the disorganization and dissipation of the self. Loneliness crops up in the modern life on account of the schism of 'tradition and individual talent'. In Maugham's realm of emancipation, the conflict operating between the 'self' and the 'real' world embroils man into the cesspool of loneliness. Maugham, unlike Eliot, is rather in pursuit of his own self. Maugham unfolds the consciousness that "was enkindled in Man as an instrument to enable him to deal with his environment and that for long ages it reached too higher development that was. needed to deal with the vital problems of his practice".[29] Maugham is truly perturbed at Man's inability to communicate to the outside world. In his various poems like 'The Waste Land' and 'The Hollowmen', Eliot laments at man's splitting up of personality. Modern Man's illusive life in which he remains shut up, says Maugham, embroils man in the endless labyrinth of loneliness. In Maugham's opinion, the "great tragedy of life is not that men perish, but that they cease to love."[30] 'April' says Eliot, no more symbolizes the life of innocence and purity. Maugham reposes his faith in 'turning loose of' the aesthetic emotions. For him the "only survival that has any value is the complete survival of the individual."[31] Maugham is disillusioned with the spiritual hollowness of the outside world, which puts obstacles to growth and unfolding of human consciousness. The 'new side' of the self has to be unfolded to retain man's individual integrity. Maugham solipsistically writes; "I must write as though I were a person of importance; and indeed, I am to my self".[32]

In 'The Painted Veil' the meaning of loneliness has been operated on the social and racial planes in which the society lies barricaded into 'us' and 'them'. Lord George who is part of the common gentry addresses the narrator with the Christian name ignoring the superciliousness, snobbery of the class consciousness and the man-made social barriers is to him, a shocking revelation; "It outraged me that he should stop me in the street and call me by my Christian name and talk to me as though there were no social difference between us."[33] Maugham thus realistically shows his concern at hypocrisies, pretensions and the false show of respectability that shut man up in mere illusion. Maugham naturalistically writes; "I do not know that the people I lived among were pretensious in the sense of making themselves out to be richer or grander than they really were, but looking back it does seem to me that they lived a life full of pretences. They dwelt behind a mask of respectability."[34] 'Desire' in his exploration of loneliness imprisons Man's 'spirit' and self-control. Man rationalistically wants to owe every object of desire to seek satisfaction. But love in Maugham's dynamics of metaphysics thrives not on satisfaction but on impediments. Strickland feels the trifling effect of desire upon man. Strickland in 'The Moon and Six Pence' experiences how desire lures him into loneliness; "I don't want love. I haven't time for it. It's weakness. I am a man, and sometimes I want a woman. When I've satisfied my passion I am ready for other things. I can't overcome my desire, but I hate it; it imprisons my spirit; I look forward to the time when I shall be free from all desire and can give myself without hindrance to my work."[35] In 'The Theatre' Julia suddenly gets awakened to the aesthetic emotion which enkindles in her a perception for seeking participation in every stance of life. Her realization of being awakened to the inertia of the self, is an exhilarating experience to her. In Maugham's realm of consciousness, the 'senses' too can play a purificatory role to cleanse the soul. The realization that she is a cog in the wheel of the theatrical establishments tragically enhances her feeling of loneliness. To Maugham, Man-Woman relationship without the aesthetic, ethical and moral values, can give no spiritual joy of domesticity; Isabel identically wants to see Larry lured into the self illusory life of Americanism. All Larry's longing for the aesthetic and esoteric life is ironically 'nothing' to her. Like Philip and Larry, Julia too feels the onslaught of the conventional ethics, Philip while living into the confines of the Blackstable comes to realize how the prevalence of the conventional ethics is devoid of the power of catering to aesthetic emotion. Every one regards Michael as a perfect husband but ironically he yokes her in the theatrical establishment to make money, power and false respectability. For Julia such a man-woman relationship is lacklustre. Her realization is tragic in the sense that the "love that had consumed her then, the jealously she had stifled, the ecstasy of surrender, it had no more reality than one of the innumerable parts she had played in the past she relished her indifference."[36] The role of the character she plays in the theatre of money, pelf and power, becomes a reflection of a own agony and exasperation. All her agony of being betrayed lured into the lack lustre marriage makes her conscious that she is a great misfit in the given circumstances. She no longer feels thrilled and elevated at her theatrical performances. She wears a dejected look feeling herself caught up and seized by her 'spirit'. She now rejoices resilience of her soul. Evie, her maid servant gives Julia a puzzled look seeing the change of heart she undergoes. Julia now is fascinated at her being awakened to the life of 'spirit'; says she, "I want to be alone and enjoy myself. Ring up Berkeley and tell them to keep a table for one in the little room. They'll know what I mean."[37]

Maugham's Naturalistic ethics is not an end but a means to emphasize the need to retrieve society from the illusive life of the 'real' world. His exploration of the dialectical art thus brings into focus the inadequacy of the real world. Maugham unlike contemporary writers doesn't discern art merely on the literal plane. In his aesthetics, greater creativity comes into being only when Man becomes conscious of the 'chaos' existing in the outside world. He can live a wholesome life of the head and heart after creating harmony between his consciousness and art. The dialectical consciousness that 'real' world man is beset with, is something akin to standing at a cross-road, becomes a stepping stone of shaping up real art, beauty and creativity. Art, as such, is a vehicle of making the inner consciousness visible in the externalities of human behaviour. Julia artistically feels; "They are our raw material. We are the meaning of their lives. We take their silly little emotions and turn them into art, out of them we create beauty, and their significance is that they form the audience we must have to fulfil ourselves. They are the instruments on which we play, and what is an instrument without somebody to play on it?"[38] Those who get disillusioned with the painted semblance of the real world, come to realize that they are artists who turn emotions into art and create beauty out of 'chaos'. Being awakened to new thrill of freedom Julia identifies herself with an artist who can create real beauty, meaning and consciousness in human life. She is now spiritually awakened to a new thrill of freedom; "Why, it's only we who do exist. They are the shadows and we give them substance. We are the symbols of all this confused, aimless struggling that they call life, and it's only the symbol which is real. They say acting is only make-believe. That make-believe is the only reality."[39] Maugham thus takes the 'real' world to be a mere semblance. He brings into focus the dialectical consciousness adding "introversion to the extroversion with which the creative instinct is inexorably associated."[40]

In Coleridge's 'The Rime of the Ancient Mariner', the meaning of loneliness has been connotated in terms of violating the ethics of the apocalyptical order. In Coleridge's realm of poetry, Man has been shown caught up in the illusive life of living a life of transgression. The loneliness depicted in his poetry is heaped upon them. A feeling of guilt consciousness and profanity wreaked up to embroil them in state of loneliness. The sailors portrayed in "The Rime of the Ancient Mariner" are made to see a 'Painted ship' on the painted surface of the sea' .The slimy creatures look horrible to them simply because they lack propensity to love all the creatures; great and small. They no longer feel themselves lonely only after they are purged of their guilt-consciousness and the deep-seated evil that possess them from within. In Eliot's 'The Family Reunion', Harry suffers from the illusion of committing murder. Harry is haunted by spirits as he carries within the burden of guilt-consciousness on the psychological plane.

Maugham thus laments at the cessation of the aesthetic and mystical realizations which end up with monotony and loneliness. The implicit conventional ethics hence, says Maugham can be made explicit and visible by dialectically spiritualising the senses.

References

1. T.S. Dorsch; Classical literary criticisim, Penguin Books, ed., p. 17.
2. W. Somerset Maugham; The Moon and Six Pence, Penguin Books Ltd., Middle Sex, England, ed., 1970, p. 180.
3. *Ibid*., p. 180.
4. *Ibid*., p. 5.
5. *Ibid*., p. 142.
6. *Ibid*., p. 140.
7. *Ibid*., p. 150.
8. G. B. Shaw, Candida, Orient Longman, Bombay, p. 81.
9. W. Somerset Maugham, The Moon and Six Pence, pp. 150-151.
10. *Ibid*., p. 150.
11. *Ibid*., p. 194.
12. *Ibid*.
13. *Ibid*., p. 174.
14. *Ibid*., p. 5.
15. *Ibid*., p. 174.
16. W. Somerset Maugham; The Painted Veil, Penguin Books, ed., 1953, p. 199.
17. p. 220.
18. *Ibid*., p. 222.
19. *Ibid*., p. 204.
20. *Ibid*., p. 224.
21. Somerset Maugham; Cakes and Ale, Penguin Books, ed., 1948, p. 158.
22. *Ibid*., p. 158.
23. *Ibid*., p. 220.
24. *Ibid*., p. 205.
25. *Op.cit.*
26. *Ibid*., p. 75.
27. *Ibid*., p. 42.
28. *Ibid*., p. 64.
29. W. Somerset Maugham, The Summing Up, p. 206

30. Ibid., p. 226.
31. *Ibid.*, p. 204
32. *Ibid.*, pp. 8-9
33. W. Somerset Maugham, Cakes and Ale, p. 69
34. *Ibid.*, p. 75
35. W. Somerset Maugham, The Moon and Sixt Pence, p. 143
36. W. Somerset Maugham, The Theartre, p. 681
37. *Ibid.*, p. 686.
38. *Ibid.*, p. 689.
39. *Ibid.*
40. W. Somerset Maugham, "Great Novelists and their novels", The John C. Winston Company Philadelphia, Toronto, ed. 1948, p. 241.

6

Of Human Bondage

Somerset Maugham's writings dialectically explore every form of human bondage. His novels, short stories and various other writings relentlessly explore the factors which cause the real crux of human bondage. The characters projected in Maugham's fictional art have been shown struggling against the odds they face in their life. The scientific and mechanical progresses man has humanistically achieved at different levels of time, says Somerset Maugham, lack the propensity to project 'deliverance' on the aesthetic and mystical planes. Thus, the projection of consciousness achieved amidst the scientific and mechanical progresses makes man a great misfit in the modern age. The rapid growth and transformation of society into the 'Brave New World', has given rise to a new collocation of human consciousness, says Maugham, needs to be addressed to retrieve man from the inclemence of human bondage. The new collocation of the modern life cropped up out of the scientific and mechanical progresses, doesn't construe to the conventional ethics. Maugham makes assertion of the basic idea that the centuries long evolution taking place at different levels of time essentially intends to liberate man from the shackles of human bondage. On the contrary the emergence of the 'Brave New World', says Huxley, causes the cessation of individuality David Daiches equates it with "the relation between loneliness and love."[1] Maugham as such, emphasizes the need to cultivate a dialectical approach in order to thwart those barricades putting obstacles to the real growth and emancipation of the homo sapiens. Marx and Engels saw man's emancipation in the dialectical materialism. Maugham instead dialectically argues that the meaning of emanciapation and 'deliverance' would remain incomplete unless man dialectically evolves a faculty to raciocinate and identify various forms of human bondage that ruthlessly push man into the throes of alienation and hedonistic pleasure. Maugham as such, emphasizes the need to cultivate empirical and rationalistic method to identify various facets of human bondage. Both the Socialistic and the Capitalistic patterns of society, says Maugham, have added new dimensions of loneliness and alienation to the orgy of the human psyche. With the relentless efforts made to emancipate man for amelioration of man in terms of the scientific, economic and mechanical developments, the inclemence of human bondage goes on to persist in society we live in. The inculcation of human suffering exists not from without but from within. Thus the need to create a world in which the 'self' is no more threatened in the alien world, finds expression in his many a novels, short stories and plays. Applying the dialectics of freedom, Maugham stresses the need to probe and see how the stark savage passions hold man in a state of bondage. P. B. Shelley, in his remarkable poem. 'Prometheus Unbound' explores the myth of human suffering. Shelley mythologically unfolds the anguish of being chained and fettered into the unperceivable knots of suffering and bondage. Maugham's characters too owe the Promethean spirit to come out of the annals of bondage by streamlining their instinctual and behaviourial patterns logistically and above all dialectically. Maugham thus creates his characters in the image whatsoever they are from within. He regards human nature as 'strange' and unknowable. The characters he creats are strange, complex, passionate, jealous and enthusiastic. His characters, as such resolve to be rationalistic. The filip side of Maugham's characters lies in their rationalistic behaviour. Their rationality lies in their empiricism and aquiesnce of knowledge in order to know the innate laws of 'truth and freedom'. Their spirit of raciocination which operates at psychic and intellectual planes, says Maugham, needs to be linked up with the aesthetic pleasure in order to address the problems caused by various forms of human bondage. In Maugham exploration of human nature, man undergoes limitless satisfaction in knowing the unknowableness of human nature. To Maugham, 'knowledge' is the vehicle of attaining freedom. Experience is the key to man's liberation from bondage. Maugham who was immensely influenced by the Indian mythology, writes, "though hardest, is the way of knowledge, for its instrument is the most precious faculty of man, his reason."[2] Maugham's characters never undergo the web of dilemma. Nor do they undergo any quandry that could shake up and embroil their grit and determination of defining their 'self. They remain fired up with the frenzy of passion to place their self in the image whatsoever they are form within. Instead of marrying Isabel, Larry prefers to remain inculcated into the dungeons of poverty and becomes one among the 'down' and 'out' in order to see how the dark savage passions play a purificatory role in cleansing man on to the hearth of human life. His harrowing experiences of discarding happiness; the glamour and glory of the 'real' world, make him aware of mystery of human bondage. Larry is lacerrated by the beastly, horrible and devastating pictures of war making him averse to attaining success. In 'The Book of Job', the unknowableness of human suffering has been depicted as it is futile to find answer to know the riddle and paradox of human suffering. Similarly Harry in T. S. Eliot's 'The Family Reunion', undergoes the illusion of committing transgression at the psychological plane. Both Philip and Larry in their own ways loiter to unburden themselves from the anguish of being guilt-conscious. The 'bright eyed' sailor in Coleridge's 'The Ancient Marimer' too like Philip and Harry is haunted by the guilt he commits by killing the albatross. Philip toils to unburden himself from all those horrible scenes which he had seen during the outbreak and conflagration of the war. Like Philip the Ancient Mariner too is haunted by the spectre of the guilt he commits by shooting the Albatross, the bird of hospitality. The horrible slimy creatures look beautiful to him only after he is spiritually cleansed by supernatural powers and is freed from guilt. The furies stop horrifying Harry only when he is made aware of the orchestration of the original sin that shrouds him in. Bertrand Russele shares Maugham's anguish of defining the self in a society which lies split up in science and metaphysics. Both Maugham and Russele in an identical way seek to find co-relation between the 'facts of science'[3] and 'mysticism'. Russele rationatically writes; "In such a nature we see the true union of the mystic and the man of science—the highest eminence as I think that it is possible to achieve in the world of thought."[4]

William Blake bifurcates human life into the songs of innocence and that of experience. In David Hume, "the scientific impluse reins quite unchecked while in Blake a strong hostility to science co-exists with profound mystical insight."[5] Edmund Spenser regards ignorance as bliss. Maugham on the other hand takes 'experience' to be the pre-requisite and a vehicle to fathom the crux of human bondage. A mere knowledge of existence of certain things and objects, says Maugham, doesn't enable man to savour the cerebral experience. Rebelling against the conventional morality, Maugham's characters projected on the dialectical canvass, experience the aesthetic emotion of despair in a bid to know their 'self' in the image they have been created. In Eliot's 'The Love song of Alfred Prufrock', women frivolusly talk of Michael Angelo without knowing the ethics and aesthetics of his art. Similarly in Eliot's 'portrait of a lady' Chopin, the polish musician who displays his art in a concert, remains a mystery to the audience. Eliot eloquently writes:

"so intimate, this Chopin, that I think his soul
should be resurrected only among friends
Some two or three, who will not touch the bloom
That is rubbed and questioned in the concert room."[6]

Eliot and Yeats see man's spiritual abberation in their hankering after the self illusory life. Maugham unlike Eliot and Yeats sees man's emancipation in applying the dialectical art, according to which man's rationalistic endeavour is ensconced with both the aesthetic and metaphysical realizations of life. Liza feels herself pretty lost in her aspiration of attaining freedom. She ironically falls prey to Jim's libido and herself paints wintry landscapes without analyzing the orgy of emotions and the inertia which make the mettle of her 'self'. Her inability to untrammel herself from her instinctual patterns of behaviour becomes her tragic flaw. Being a prisoner of her own 'impulse' she rather gets entrapped. Pitted against a situation in which she is to opt either for Tom or for Jim; She impulsively yields to Jim's libido and gets tragically sombre. The fireworks of the basic instincts make her essentially indifferent to the ethical and aesthetic values which put obstacles to her achieving emancipation from the mundane life. Sally who symbolises the voice of sanity and reason reminds Liza of her falling into the impulse. Liza doesn't gain consciousness unless her self illusory life jeopardizes all her hopes of attaining emancipation. Maugham in an identical way, feels himself bewildered at the way the modern generation is swallowed by the hedonistic and the illusory life. Facing the illusiveness of the 'real' life, Maugham applies a more pragmatic vision to subdue the impulse. Philip in 'Of Human Bondage', feels; "They must discover for themselves that all they have been told are lies, lies, lies: each discovery is another nail driven into the body on the cross of life. The strange thing is that each one who has gone through that bitter disillusionment adds to it in his turn, unconsciously, by the power within him which is stronger than himself'[7]. Liza lacks insight and clairvoyance to see that her bondage to the impulse she has within, lay in her yielding to Jim's jarring notes of love. In his another novel, 'The Magician', Maugham explores that Kafkayesque experience of the belittleness of man. The evil, Maugham exposes in Hado, is indicative of the innate and the deep-seated human depravity. Hado who is an embodiment of human depravity, conjures up the incantatory spells to cater to his hedonistic pursuit of life. Maugham thus exposes the perversity of the evil which remains deep-seated in man. Margaret is made to yield to the 'Black' art which Hado practises. Arthur, doesn't comprehend the paradox of life and goes on to love Margarate without noticing the change which had cropped up in her. Thus, Maugham like Forster dialectically argues that both the good and evil remain sacrosanct and inseparable from each other. The deep-seated evil which lies inherent in man, says Maugham, can't be dismantled unless the dialectical approach to life is applied. Margarate herself feels condescending under the incantatory and hideous spell. Hado who is devil incarnate and a symbol of repugnance, conjures her up and seizes her soul through his incatatory spells to hold her in 'bondage'. There is nothing in Margaret that could awaken in her the sanity to escape from Hado's hedonism. Hado is a prototype of Shakespeare's Iago. He practises black art to bring her under his hypnotic spell. Iago too under the spell of mad jealousy utters; "I am not what I am."[8] Maugham's characters thus lack perspicacity to look into the shape of things to come. They go on to remain caught up into the self-illusory life Arthur who lacks clairvoyance and empathy to look into the after-effects of putting off his marriage that could trundle the apple cart of their life making his freedom elude to him. Prohoet like sally who is the voice of reason, utilises his rationalistics to make Arthur aware of the disastrous consequences of putting off the marriage. War leaves Larry in a horribly devastating experience. He walks tiptoe on to the 'the razor's edge' to cater to his needs of aesthetic sensibility in order to evolve a philosophy that could spiritualize reason. Isabel who is devastated at Larry's resolution to do 'nothing' but loiter, shakes her up from within. To her Larry has 'nothing' to do but except that he should live up to the expectations of the life of"Americanism' in which money is put up for supplication and raised to the elevation of 'money-god'. Eliot, in an identical way laments at the delusion and self-illusory life of the modern man in which 'the stone images' are raised for supplication. Eliot symbolically writes;

"Here the stone images
Are raised, here they receive
The supplication of a dead man's hand
under the twinkle of a fading star"[9]

In Eliot's 'The Wasteland', the Wastelanders and the hollowmen have been regarded as deadening spirits; a spectre of chaos and confusion. Living listlessly, Larry beholds no beauty in the machanics of the modern world. Isabel on the contrary is all aglow; replete with the fire and brim stones to live up to the expectations what 'Americanism' means for. For Larry to yield to a life what 'Americanism' means for is something akin to 'the betrayal of the soul'. Isabel on the other hand shows repugnance to Larry's luck-lustre response to her livid emotions. Isabels says; "All this is just triffling. It's not going to lead you anywhere. For your own sake I beseech you to give up. Be a man, Larry, and do a man's work. You're just wasting the precious years that others are doing so much with Larry, if you love me you won't give me up for a dream, you have had your fling. Come back with us to America."[10] No sooner does Julia get aware of the throbbing of her 'self' than her aesthetic yearning for coming out of the 'theatre' of the hedonistic and lascivious entrapment that intends to make man 'be all and end all' in his search of happiness. The epiphany Maugham employs in his fictional art brings into focus the images of flow and the images of flight to unrol not only his cherished desires of attaining freedom but also, it shows up the anguish of the soul; frizzled and frazzled to get man unentwined from the cocoon of human bondage. Julia feels the thrill of freedom within her; "She had a wonderful sense of freedom form all earthly ties, and it was such an ecstasy that nothing in comparison with it had any value she felt like a spirit in heaven."[11] Julia-Michael relationship moves about in different directions. They speak out their anguish in different tones and tenors. Julia grows conscious of the monotonous overtures of the theatre. Realising that she has been made part of the theatrical skill to display her theatrical performances for making Michael's desires meet both ends, gives her Jerks and Jolts. Her anguish of being caught up and getting inculcated into the lack-lustre theatrical life, makes her realise that the threatrical life for which she was lured into, proves itself the alienation of her own self. The basic instinct of defining her 'self' in the real world, makes her spirit thrilled with a new sensation of attaining emancipation. Her every act of theatrical performances that leads to her materialistic and hedonistic life, ends with a fuss; she comes to realise that everything which glitters is not beautiful. Like Gray Matruin, Isabel takes life to be a mere vehicle of deriving happiness. She lacks insight and clairvoyance to see meaning, pattern and design in the human existence. On the other hand Gray Matruin who equates life in terms of premium, ironically becomes tragic, has nothing within him to behold the 'beautiful' in the real world existing outside him.

Like E. M. Foster, Maugham explicates the paradox of evil. The exposition of evil in Maugham's world is 'as direct manifestation of the divine as good.'[12] The Naturalistic ethics in Maugham's framework of the dialectical art presents the wholesomeness of both the good and evil. Like Conrad Maugham too believes that from the evil emanates the good. Kurtz's confession of the unspeakable "The horror! The horror!"[13] transforms him into a better human being enkindling in him hope and renovation of a life of spirits. Maugham in an identical way, dialectically argues that a life of 'experience' becomes a threshold of the dynamics of the aesthetic, metaphysical and mystical aspects. When the evil recedes, says Forster, the good implicit in man becomes explicit. In Forster's A passage to India, the multicultural and the multiracial society goes on to remain in a state of bondage unless man achieves deliverance from the culture-shock, descrimination and hatred. In 'The Painted Veil', Maugham brings into focus the hidden malignancy and repugnance clamped in the colonial society. The natives of the 'painted veil' of the 'real' world, wear a resigned look; unconcerned with the politics of descrimination. Their stoicism and indifference to their plight has nothing to do with the suffering heaped upon them. It is Mother Superior who creates in Kitty the power of striking a balance between 'love' and 'duty'. For Maugham beauty 'alone can discover the realm of truth and freedom. Instead the element of 'pleasure' acts as a moving force to make the conventional ethics dynamic and operative. 'Beauty' sans 'pleasure' says Somerset Maugham, presents incomplete picture of human life making the conventional ethics inoperative in the true sense. Philip while living in Blackstable, feels no way out to aesthetically define the self he has from within. Everything he beholds looks hostile and threatening to his self. In the painted veil, Sister Francis infuses in Kitty the faith that enkindles in her hope and optimism; "And then Sister Francis Xavier—that in the name of the Sister who died last night—took my hand and told me not to grieve; for wherever we were she said, there was France and there was God."[14] Thus the characters projected on the dialectical plane, work as the objective co-relative to connotate the apocalyptical meaning of the human existenance. The pole in Maugham's 'The Razor Edge', explicates the conundrum of the human existence finding pattern, design, and symphony therein. Both good and evil says the Pole, are part of the apocalypse of unfolding the riddle of human life in totality. The Pole says "that the world isn't a creation, for out of nothing comes; but a manifestation of the eternal nature; well, that was all right, but then he added that evil is as direct a manifestation of the divine as good. They were strange words to hear in that sordid, noisy cafe, to the accompaniment of dance tunes on the mechanical piano."[15]

Oscar Wilde takes 'pleasure' to be the basic driving force for the human endeavour in his search of freedom. Establishing relation between man and nature Wilde says that it is Nature which manifests itself in man through 'pleasure'. Eliot in his significant 'essay', Frontiers of criticism, puts emphasis on the inter-connection of enjoyment and understanding saying that understanding and enjoyment are complementary to each other. Maugham too emphasizes the inter-connection of aesthetic beauty and pleasure. Maugham streamlines the elements of art, pleasure and morality while creating a work of art. Maugham thus syllogestically explores the naunces of beauty and basically discerns that the three logical propositions—art, pleasure and morality remain ensconced with one another. To scuttle the elements of pleasure from Maugham's ethical paradigms, is tantamount to put aside the soul and organity unity of a work of art pleasure prevents a work of art from disassociation of sensibility. Man's inability to spiritualise the web of reason, says Maugham thus constitutes human bondage in the modern world. Liza commits error in yielding to her impulse. Her impulsive relationship with Jim makes upside down the apple cart of all her hope of coming out of the mundane life. The enthusiasm to break the bond of the mundane and ethereal life, no more lifts her to a state of renovation. Everything looks, pale, lack-lustre and rudimentry to her. Kitty aesthetically regains consciousness after. She becomes aware of her lack-lustre relation with Walter. The pain of loneliness tears her apart; the realisation of undergoing a state of bondage, infuses in her a sense of vacancy; the anguish that totally shakes up her nerves—making her conscious of a 'new' awakening. Thus the new thrill of translating the dream of freedom into a concrete reality in Kitty makes her envision a renewed hope, comeliness and aesthetic beauty. Maugham regards beauty as "a gift of God, one of the most rare and precious, and we should be thankful if we are happy enough to possess it and thankful, if we are not, that others possess it for our pleasure."[16] Kitty learns wisdom and the mystery of greater faith from the experience she passess through as well as from the sisters of charity. Greater faith to Kitty lies not in hankering after the illusive life of happiness, instead it lies in the purity of the soul as well as in rendering service to the mankind. She feels the inertia of her self and realizes; "It is not faith, it is something deeper and more—more significant: they walk in different world from ours and we shall always be strangers to them. Each day when the convent door closes behind me I feel that for them I have ceased to exist."[17] 'Beauty' in Maugham's domain of freedom is thus a liberating force to elevate man to the terrace of transcendence. In The Moon and Six pence the narrater explicates the cleansing power of beauty. Maugham writes; "Beauty is something wonderful and strange that the artist fashions out of the chaos of the world in the torment of his soul. And when he has made it, it is not given to all to know it. To recognize it you must repeat the adventure of the artist. It is a melody that he sings to you, and to hear it again in your own heart you want knowledge and sensitiveness and imagination."[18] Shaw was an iconoclast who applied the instrument of realism to bring man out of the shackles of the romantic sensibility. As H.G. Wells assumed science to be dismantling the ills of society, Shaw, on the other hand, regarded realism as an instrument of removing all the impoverishment that made man economally wretched. In 'Mrs. Warren's profession' Shaw holds the economic deprivation and poverty to be the crucial factors behind the suffering meted out to man. Maugham apart from Wells and Shaw applies the dialectal art to retrieve man from the illusive life he lives in the modern context. In a similar way Eugene Marchbanks in Shaw's 'Candida' wants to take Candida where the stars look like lamps; "No, Not a scrubbing brush; but a tiny shallop to sail away in, far from the world, where the marble floors are washed by the rain and dried by the sun, where the south wind dusts the beautiful green and purple carpets. Or a chariot! to carry us up into the sky, where the lamps stars, and don't need to be filled with paraffin oil everyday."[19] Morell is a socialist clergyman who makes beautiful and metaphorical speeches but ironically he himself remains alien to the finer naunces of morality. Morell makes Candida grub the floor and do menial work. Eugene Marchbanks' romantic sensibility receives jerks and Jolts seeing Candida's fingers dabbled in paraffin oil. William Carey like Morell, makes people do the customery into the confines of Blackstable. Ironically the Vicar of Blackstable is stranger to the finer perceptions of aesthetic beauty, the aesthetic beauty which moves up and makes the conventional ethics functional and operative. The cessation of the applied ethics—the casuistry, prevailing in Blackstable makes philip feel alien in his owns surroundings. He feels himself embroiled at the abstract morality which ceases the aesthetic perception of life resulting in the pacifism and cessation of spirituality. The experience of being made to fall in line with the conventional ethics, creates a consciousness for flight from the mundane life which stifles and annihilates all the humanistic endeavour man applies for achieving freedom. Maugham writes:

"But he had grown very self-conscious. The new-born child does not realise that his body is more a part of himself than surrounding objects, and will play with his toes without any feeling that they belong to him more than the rattle by his side; and it is only by degrees, through pain, that he understands the fact of the body. And experiences of the same kind are necessary for the individual to become conscious of himself; but here there is the difference that, although everyone becomes equally conscious of his body as a separate and complete organism, everyone does not become equally conscious of himself as a complete and separate personality."[20] In Maugham's dialectics of freedom, knowledge, sensitiveness and imagination thus get streamlined into one organic whole.

In Maugham's dynamics of freedom the 'body' and soul remain inter-related. The consciousness of the bodily and cerebral experiences creates in man a new being in order to get man detached from the social, political, economic and racial constraints. The humiliation borne to Philip in King's school makes him essentially conscious of his throbbing self. Philip like Stephen Dedalus rebels against the sinister designs of society where suppression of the self in the alien world, makes his spirit sealed with all its apathy. Philip aspires for having himself unentwined from every form of bondage; the bondage that captivates and seizes up the human soul. Similarly Kitty resolves to flight from the sordid realities of life. She identifies herself with a phoenix getting incarnated out of the ashes of her own mundane life of experience. For Michael Julia is a means to earn laurels of pelf and power. Being put up on to the pedestal of the theatre, she is made a vehicle of earning name and fame, money power and respectability. Michael who is too much obsessed with the spiritually hollow life of the theatre lives an illusive life in which both Roger and Julia are treated with apathy. His escape to America to live a life of 'satiety' on the rationalistic plane, pushes him in to the endless labyrinth of loneliness. William Carey in 'Of Human Bondage' puts himself up in oblivion. Human life to him is nothing but a paraphernalia of rituals one should not trespass. Thus man projected on Maugham's dialectical canvas, has been shown aspiring for coming up the life of bondage.

Maugham's characters thus thrive on their inability to live a live of satiety. Like Shaw, Maugham deals with the theme of love and matrimony. Love in Maugham's dialectical art, is not a spent up force; instead it achieves transcendence and spiritual elevation. Michael's love for Julia becomes a sacrilege as she is made an object of the theatre of the absurd. Like Kurtz's utterences of unspeakable 'The horror! The horror',[21] Kitty undergoes the agony of the cerebral experience and makes confession of the deep seated evil that embroils her in loneliness: she curls up in agony and remorse; "It was curious to go into her own house as though she were a stranger."[22] The realization of being guilt conscious makes her averse to her ownself. The cathartic process operating within raises herself above the social, political and racial constraints transforming her into a better human being.

What Maugham dialectically aspires for is a greater reality to retrieve man from the inclemence of human bondage. Maugham is concerned at exploring every form of human bondage that puts the human spirit in chains. Philip's mother finds life a blind alley at her death bed. Blackstable bullies Philip and stifles his soul. In Maugham's exploration of human bondage, the concept of white man's burden has been linked up with a society in which love and duty become one. In Kipling's bazar, the concept of the white man's burden is not just made limited to the zeal of cherishing the cause of the natives. Maugham unlike Kipling doesn't take the responsibility of championing the cause of the natives as 'burden' instead in Maugham's realm of freedom the concept of the white man's burden is extended to and made part of 'love' and 'duty'. Mother Superior in 'The Painted Veil' comes up to Kitty with a new meaning of freedom; wherein man no more lives with the trauma of carrying the white man's burden. Instead Maugham's dialectics of freedom is an intermingling of 'love' and 'duty'. In 'Cakes and Ale' Maugham delineates a new morality breaking new grounds for defining the self in the outside world. He employs the dialectical art to cut across the prevailing pretensions and man-made bariers. Maugham shows his aversion to compartmentalization of society into 'you' and 'they'. As Maugham is essentially a rebel, the 'reason' in him evokes a sense of universal brotherhood in which man is no more disgruntled for being part of the humanity. Man's aspiration for getting retrieved from the onslaught of alienation and spiritual crisis— is thus demonstrative of the anguish of soul for greater freedom. Stephen Dedalus, in an identical way resolves to get retrieved from the life of bondage humanistically. Maugham's characters never bring catacalysmic change to their self nor do they make compromises with the 'real' and the illusive life. The trauma of being treated with apathy by the conventional ethics is something akin to 'mocking absurdity tied to a dog's tail'[23] Blackstable is a hostile place where everything is dealt with the parameter of the conventional morality. The petty squabbles taking place in the day-to-day affairs of Paris enhance the pitch of loneliness. Plato in his 'Republic' had dabbled his hands in fires by banishing poets from the ideal republic. Maugham has his own ideals of republic. The search for art, morality, beauty and comeliness, to Maugham, has more significance than hankering after the illusive life of happiness. Hence escape from the alien society to achieve fulfilment at the literary, artistic, aesthetic, metaphysical and spiritual planes, brings solace to the characters Maugham's creates. Philip's escape to Paris is part of his search for a world catering to the 'spirits'. All Philip's extravaganza for a philosophy to cater to the needs of art, beauty and religion is the basic thrust on which his search for achieving greater freedom rests. Maugham shows his despair at the enormity of the mechanistic society in which man is a mere prisoner of his own masochistic desires. Maugham says that emotion of multitude and the impulse which remain inherent in the being of man are themselves a greater reality. John Donne's concept of beauty is thus wholesomely associated with the idea of truth and beauty. In the post modern literature, man has basically been shown conscious of his frantic search for creating a new space to define the stance of life. No sooner does man become aware of his 'new' being than he becomes pre-occupied and obsessed with the idea of attaining freedom from the mundane and ethereal life. It is man's proneness to yield to passion which holds him in a state of bondage. Living a life of materialistic pursuit is what crops up human bondage to passion. It is in this sense that 'London' in Eliot's 'The Wasteland' has been regarded as the 'unreal' city. Maugham allows his characters to emerge on his dialectical plane making the subjective objective. Maugham thus dialectically says that in each character, passion acts as a tragic flaw making man essentially conscious of the need to achieve transcendence and liberation from bondage, social constraints and illusion. As such Philip at length grows relationship with Miss Wilkinson, Fanny Price, Nesbit, Heyward, Cronshaw and above all Mildred; in each character the 'passion' to achieve liberation, entwines Man into the endless labyrinth of human bondage. His escape to Germany and his encounter-with the Frau daughters creates in him clairvoyance to distinguish between 'happiness' and pleasure enabling him to perceive the real world with the aesthetic and ethical imagination. G. H. Mair hence rightly says; "Somerset Maugham found it harder to control his antipathy than to check his sympathies. Sympathy relaxes, antipathy braces, it therefore follows that Somerset Maugham's work is highly invigorating particularly as an irritant to those who are antipathic to his own antipathies. This feature of his work is most evident in his short stories and in "The Moon and Six Pence". There is a fuller and rounder view of the world in the long novel of human bondage in which in his master piece, Cakes and Ale, and adorable Rosie is enchantingly shaped in an embracing matrix of the author's antipathies."[24]

Unlike Wells and Shaw, Maugham doesn't connotate human bondage in terms of the suffering and economic deprivation taking place on the physical plane. The consciousness which remains at work says Maugham, creates in Man the Power of perceiving various forms of human bondage. Maugham is enthused with the Promethean spirit to take Man out of the tentacles of bondage which seize up and fetters the human spirit. He applies the dialectics of aesthetic sensibility to take Man from the state of experience to that of emancipation. The anguish to put up his stance of life in the alien surroundings receives impetus to explore varied forms of human bondage. Maugham is not bemused at the colossal growth of intellect instead he aesthetically argues that the 'senses' too can play a purificatory role in cleansing the soul. The Cathartic emotions on account of man's living a life of impulse seizes up his soul in bondage. Man's inability to co-relate the enormity of scientific facts with the aesthetic emotion, gives vent to explore areas of human bondage. The real 'tragedy of life' from Maugham's dialectical perspective, is not that men perish but they cease to love".[25]

Maugham's characters remain imprisoned into the tentacles of human bondage. They are a product of their being. Man says Maugham, has proneness to be entrapped by impulse and the illusiveness of the real world. The conflict operating between impulse and reason, says he, is one of the factors which constitute human bondage. The exploration of human bondage itself enkindles in Man a faculty to take Man to the road of freedom. Man would go on to suffer unless he envisages the consciousness that remains invisible to him. It is in this perspective to which probes various forms of human bondage persisting in the post modern era. As such he regards man's alienation, rootlessness and his search for identity as a by-product of his inability to correlate with thc aesthetic emotion. It is the art of the invisible; the area of consiousness which is more significant than Man's running in a blind alley in pursuit of the happiness existing in the outside world. Maugham thus stands closer tó Flaubert, Balzac and D.H. Lawrence. He aesthetically studies the root-cause of man's despair and begins his journey of inquisition of man's despair and melancholy from the consciousness itself. Eliot at the very outset quizzically looks at the spiritually disorganized modern life and says that tragedy lies ensconced in Man's alienation from the spiritual and ethical order. Eliot ignores the aesthetic verse and doesn't explicate how the modern trends like alienation crops up in the mindset of the wastelanders. Maugham on the other hand, delves deep into the crux of human bondage pointing out at the schism that exists between the self and the outside world. He solipsistically defines the aesthetic stance of life opening up new horizons to the new side of the self which remains invisible to the real world. What he basically argues that all human aspirations would remain incomplete unless Man in the Modern World envisages a faculty of identifying various forms of human bondage. 'Survival of the individual' says

Maugham alone can take Man out of human bondage. Thus Maugham elaborates the mechanics of the aesthetic emotion which sweeps Man from bondage to emancipation.

As Maugham is ethically conscious of the pitfalls of living the illusive life, he elaborates the dialectical art to make the dysfunctional conventional ethics operative by streamlining the enormous growth of scientific facts with the aesthetic emotion. Thus the dialectical consciousness, says Maugham is the know how according to which evolutionary and scientific developments remain associated with aesthetic sensibility is—syllogistically capable of making the abstract conventional ethics operative. Characters projected on the canvas of Maugham's dialectical art long for emancipation from their bondage to the abstract and in-operative conventional ethics. Liza Lambeth hopes for renovation of spirit; her thrills and sensation of freedom end with Jarring notes after she gives in to her impulse. Liza-Jim Blackeston relationship shows how Man's falling prey to libido enchains Man in bondage and servility. Julia gets spiritually awakened to the futility of her own life. She contemplates that the World is a stage and men and women mere players. On the one hand, she becomes aware of the otherness of the 'real' world in which man runs after illusive life. On the other hand her realization that the actors symbolize illusion, meaninglessness and their futility enables her to draw a line of bifurcation between 'us' and 'they'. Julia comes to realize that the characters performing onto the stage are the real artists in the sense that they create art out of chaos and desultoriness. The consciousness deep-seated in her enables her to learn how she has been a 'plaything'; an object of desire in her giving performances in the theatrical world. She becomes aesthetically conscious of the 'new side' of man-woman relationship. She grows tired of the man-woman relationship which is to her not only soulless but also perfunctory. Maugham projects man with all his proneness to yield to her temptation, impulse and to the seven ambiguites which condescend Man from within. Maugham at the same time addresses the problem of security. Attainment of the glamour and glory Julia gets by virtue of her performing in the theatrical establishments, hardly could give her security and a sense of belonging. Getting awakened to a new spirit of freedom, she comes to realize that the aesthetic emotion surging within her after all can't be subdued. Thus the need of security, goes on to prevail in the inner recesses of the human consciousness. "She was free of the bondage in which her senses had held her to him and she exulted"[26] In the 'painted veil' of the 'real' world, Kitty no more feels herself secure in the racially hostile society. Being unable to communicate to the outside world, she remains a mere prisoner in the alien surroundings. Philip, in 'Of Human Bondage' runs frantically from one human predicament to another. The conventional ethics he is beset with, provides him no sense of belonging. Philip develops a series of relationships with characters like Miss Wilkinson, Fanny Price, Heyward, Cornshaw and Week and Mildred in order to see the 'real' world in the image they have been created. Philip paints wintry landscapes in his passionate yielding to Mildred. The larger is the degree of proclivity to her the greater is his bondage and servility to passion. In Maugham's domain of human bondage, Yielding to passion results in bondage whereas getting unentwined from passion is freedom. Fanny price who believes in her 'self' with all her heart, knows no rationality to come out of her bondage to passion. Thus each and every character utilizes his consciousness creates a world of his own that could give him a sense of belonging in the modern context. It is the sense of belonging which Philip craves for while living into the confines of Blackstable. Thus 'Survival of the self' says Maugham alone can retrieve man from the intricacies of human bondage. He elaborates the mechanics of the human consciousness and the aesthetic emotion which sweeps Man from bondage to emancipation. As he believes in the gospel of the apocalypse he elaborates the dialectical art to point out at the inadequacies of the conventional ethics. The dialectical art which links up the evolutionary and scientific facts with the aesthetic sensibility—is syllogistically capable of making the conventional ethics operative. Maugham is equally conscious of the inadequacy of both dialectical materialism and western cult of emancipating Man from bondage. Maugham never looses grip on consciousness that establishes a harmonious relation between the self and the outside world. Through the portrayal of Philip, Larry, Kitty and Liza Lambeth, he explains the dialectical consciousness that the 'painted veil' of the 'real' world is ironically devoid of the power to create art, beauty and creativity in the true sense. Julia takes her consciousness to be the only reality that could envision art, beauty and creativity. Being conscious of the illusion of the outside world, she feels; "She had a wonderful sense of freedom from all earthly ties, and it was such an ecstasy that nothing in comparison with it had any value she felt like a spirit in heaven."[27] Liza Lambeth in an identical way finds herself caught up in a strange situation. Her lack of consciousness that yielding to the otherness of the self, embroils her in a life of bondage. The realization that she has been made to yield to impulse sharpens her feeling of loneliness in the outside world. Hence all the evolutionary, scientific experiences and amelioration made to achieve emancipation of the homo sapiens would remain futile unless a dialectical approach to which the rationalistic and aesthetic aspects remain ensconced, can alone emancipate Man from bondage. All the high profile slogans of emancipating man from the prevalence of bondage says Maugham, would remain incomplete if he remains oblivious of the doctrine of the inner self. Man with all his endeavour for taking refuge in dialectical materialism feels himself apprehensive of being dislocated from the aesthetic mainstream of life. Maugham had a little faith in altruistic means of emancipating man. He unflinchingly believes that the consciousness inherent in the inner recesses of the human psyche is directly inter-related with 'survival of the individual'. Hence, Maugham's dialectical art opens up a new horizon, a third space to stream line all the rationalistic aspirations with the aesthetic sensibility. Real emancipation exists not in the socio-political realizations says he; instead it is the implicit consciousness which alone unfolds various avenues of emancipating man from the state of human bondage. Maugham is thus a terribly religious artist who is conscious of the illusion and hypocrisy of the 'real' society, evokes a sense of belonging in order to define his 'self' in the outside world in the image he has been created. It can be aesthetically evinced that Maugham is in pursuit of his 'self'. Eliot on the other hand builds up his theory of art on 'escape of emotion' and 'extinction personality'; Maugham on the other hand clings to 'turning loose' of the aesthetic emotion in the externalities of human behaviour. Unlike Marcel Proust, Dorothy Richardson and Virginia Woolf, Maugham does not believe in exploring the psychoanalytical interpretation of the human psyche, he on the other hand makes the doctrine of the inner self the basis on which he projects a co-relation between the ever widening human consciousness and the aesthetic sensibility.

References

1. David Daiches; A Critical History of English Literature, Vol. IV, Revised edition, Allied Publishers Limited, New Delhi, 1994, p. 1171.
2. W. Somerset Maugham; The Razor's Edge, p. 512.
3. Bertrand Russell; Mysticism and logic and other essays, p. 10.
4. *Ibid*., p. 11.
5. *Ibid*., p. 9.
6. T.S. Eliot; 'Portrait of a Lady', Selected poems. p. 17.
7. W. Somerset Maugham; Of Human Bondage, p. 144.
8. William Shakespeare; Othello, The Complete works, The English Language Book Society and Collins, London and Glasgow, ed. 1964 p. 1115.
9. T.S. Eliot; Selected poems, The Hollowmen, p. 78.
10. W. Somerset Maugham; The Razor's Edge, p. 386.
11. W. Somerset Maugham; The Theatre, p. 689.
12. *Ibid*., p. 406.
13. Joseph Conrad; The Heart Of Darkness, Surjeet Publications, New Delhi ed., 1988 p. 100.
14. W. Somerset Maugham; The Painted Veil, p. 132.
15. W. Somerset Maugham; The Razor's Edge, p. 406.
16. W. Somerset Maugham; Painted Veil, p. 145.
17. *Ibid*., p. 148.
18. W. Somerset Maugham; The Moon and Six Pence, p. 72.
19. G.B. Shaw; Candida, p. 5.
20. W. Somerset Maugham; Of Human Bondage, p. 54.
21. Joseph Conard; *op.cit.*

22. W. Somerset Maugham; The Painted Veil, p. 222.
23. W.B. Yeats; The Tower, p. 105.
24. G. H. Mair; Modern English Literature, Oxford University Press, London, ed., 1956, p. 220.
25. W. Somerset Maugham; The Summing up, p. 226.
26. W. Somerset Maugham; The Theatre, p. 577.
27. *Ibid.*, p. 689.

7
Search for Freedom

Maugham's dialectical approach to life rationalises the humanistic urges to unchain man from the onslaught of human bondage. It rationalistically streamlines the impulsive and instinctual patterns of behaviour which inculcates man into the endless cesspool of loneliness. Maugham's characters are moved up by the idea of the 'beautiful'; the aesthetic perception which gives them the power of differentiating between the sacred and the profane. The cult of attaining the life of materialistic progress then no more remains significant to them. Maugham's dialectical approach to life rationalises the innate, dark and savage passions giving a new aesthetic perception to man. The new impetus thrust by the aesthetic perception, opens up new horizons of freedom as it protects man from being machine-like. Being caught up into the web of the savage passions, man says, Somerset Maugham, finds himself inculcated into a state of bondage. By applying a dialectical approach to life Maugham thus brings into focus various forms of bondage and depravity which persist in society. Maugham hence dialectically argues that every human endeavour applied for attaining emancipation, would remain incomplete unless man involves a rationalistic power to identify various forms of human bondage. It is this implied dialectical approach says Somerset Maugham that enables man to reason and identify varied iota of human bondage. Utilising the dynamics of dialecticism, Maugham makes man aware of the illusion of materialistic pursuit of life. Maugham's characters never look back and make compromises even after menacingly restrained by the hostile and alienating world. They go on to pin their hope of renovation by aesthetically defining their stance of life in the din and bustle of the mechanical world. The innate and deep seated stark passions enkindle in man a new aesthetic and spiritual perception in which man God and the world get streamlined in one cosmic vision. It is a homogenous state in which man is no longer existentially threatened by travails of the mechanical set up. Maugham thus basically argues how the modern world with all its scientific and technological jargons fallaciously promise to retrieve man from the inclemence of human bondage merely on the physical plane. Anthony Curtis defends Maugham's emphasis of aesthetic beauty in a work of art; "Maugham learns about the problems involved in representing the quality of light and distortion of human form in the interest of greater realisation."[1]

This shows that Maugham is conscious of the instincts and the impulses which are themselves part of the greater reality, seek their participation in every behavioural pattern. Thus the life of experience in Maugham's concept of transcendence and liberation is essentially a vehicle of linking the humanistic and evolutionary up with the metaphysics of love. Maugham is not appalled and bemused at the colossal upsurge of the scientific and rationalistic growth of society. It is in this sense that Maugham has a scientific temper to look into the alienation and pessimism in order to bring all the scientific developments to the fold of metaphysics and its spirituality. Elaborating the applied ethics, Maugham dialectically believes that all the scientific and atomic collocations projected during the evolutionary processes, need to be spiritualised taking into account those basic instincts which excruciatingly play up their participation in the evocativeness of the self. Thoman. H. Huxley, in his essay, 'Evolution and ethics' like Maugham too believes that the "The faith which is born of knowledge, finds its objects in an eternal order, bringing forth ceaseless change, through endless time, in endless space, the manifestation of the cosmic energy alternating between phases of potentiality and phases of explication."[2] The materialistic cult of achieving 'happiness' brought about by the 'scientific romance' ironically turns into nightmare and dissipation of the 'self'. In 'The Picture of Dorian Gray' Wilde shows the conflict between aesthetic beauty and intellect and opines that 'the true mystery in the world is the visible not the invisible'.[3]

Maugham's characters are fired up with the zest to define their stance of life in the alienating society. It is the aesthetic perception which embues them with a new thrill of freedom in order to come up their life of bondage. In Maugham's 'The Razor's Edge' Larry loiters around and does 'nothing'[4] but 'loaf'[5]. Fired up under spell of the dark savage passions, he forsakes the life of 'Americanism' according to which success is taken to be the touchstone of 'happiness', Larry unties the knots of betrothal to Isabel, goes down into the dungeons of poverty and becomes one among the 'down and out'. The fury of passions implicit in him cleanses him from within and opens up floodgates of aesthetic perception of beauty. From Maugham's standpoint, 'beauty' lies in the aesthetic perception of the beholder.

The horrible experiences Larry passes through during the war, make himself aware of the need to see the world in the image of the self. Maugham thus applies the doctrine of the casuistry, the applied ethics to place man in the image of the 'self'. In 'Of Human Bondage' Philip is an insider outsider who can't afford to fall in line with the conventional ethics. Man in the modern world, says Maugham, adores and adheres to the happiness principle. Maugham thus ethically opines that man who frantically runs after the hedonistic life in the 'Brave New World', ironically doesn't afford to come up the cult of happiness. The dialectical vision thus opens a horizons of aesthetic and mystical revelation of beauty giving him impetus to renounce the 'happiness' they remain wrapped up with. A new role of reason intermingled with the aesthetic values alone can open up, says Maugham, the horizon of freedom. Hence Maugham by his applied ethics, emphasizes the need to explore the mettle of man in the image of the self which to him basically builds up the being of man. Isabel whom Larry is betrothed to, gets surprised at the way Larry denies taking happiness in both his hands. Instead, he acts violating the mainstream of the concierge of happiness and wants to do 'nothing'. Larry is thus a prototype to Cordelia who takes 'nothing' from her father. Lear is unaware of the meaning and connotation of 'human bondage', as he hasn't ever come across with it, haughtily outbursts; "Nothing will come out of Nothing".[6] In the Shakespearian domain of the theatrical skills, suffering emanates from the protagonist's proclivity to his tragic flaw. On the other hand, in Somerset Maugham's realm of tragedy, the dark and elemental savage passions bind man to the unabated and relentless suffering. This is how the flamboyance of emotions do to Larry and

Philip. For Larry, acting against the conventional ethics could unbind him from the bestiality of the cult of 'happiness' which end up with the cropping of the 'Brave New World'. Man in the 'Brave New World', says Aldous Huxley, is ironically unaware of how the 'tether' of 'happiness' pushes man into the endless labyrinth of loneliness. Eliot laments at the ingrained alienation which crops up within the human psyche. Man's craving for coming out of the clioster of the illusive life, says Eliot, is something akin to throwing the key and hoping for coming out of the illusive life of the 'prison'. Eliot thus laments at the plight of the modern man as he runs desultorily after the worldly and the mechanical life. Eliot symbolically writes;

> "I have heard the key
> Turn in the door once and turn once only
> We think of the key, each in his prison
> Thinking of the key, each confirms a prison
> Only at nightfall, aethereal rumours
> Revive for a moment a broken Coriolanus".[7]

The scientific facts, says Maugham, are themselves tinged with a greater reality and the concept of freedom comes full circle only when the colossal growth of science is brought to the spiritual and metaphysical fold. The aesthetic beauty which Maugham paints with all its shades and designs focus those areas of primeval beauty which creates in man an awakening for attaining freedom from the mundane world. Liza Lambeth in the beginning has been shown dancing in a state of frenzy, is indicative of the vision of emancipation which looms large to her, functions within to transmute the inertia of the self into action. Oscar Wilde like Maugham emphasizes a complete harmony of the body and soul; flesh and spirit. Getting influenced by the external behaviour, says Wilde, violates the ethics of the soul. Wilde writes; "To be good is to be in harmony with one's self," he replied, touching the thin stem of his glass with his pale, fine-pointed fingers. "Discord is to be forced to be in harmony with others. One's own life—that is the important thing".[8] It is this frenzy for attaining freedom from the life of fret and fever, for which Maugham's character move about, shows how William Carey hardly cares for the anguish Philip undergoes and feels his 'self stifled into the confines of the Blackstable. Nor is Philip allowed to define his self the way he aesthetically aspires for. In Dickens' novel 'Hard Times', Tom and Louisa suffocatingly feel their self thwarted as they aren't allowed to enter the Alice's Wonderland. Philip's feeling are no different from those of Stephen Dedalus who in an identical way is made to go through inflictment and loneliness. "O, if not, the eagles will come and pluck out his eyes"[9] shows how harshly he is made to fall in line with the conventional ethics. Philip's feelings are no different from those of Stephen Dedalus who in an identical way is made to go through the pain of loneliness. Maugham's characters thus define the stance of life in the image of whatsoever they are from within. Philip Carey like Stephen Dedalus is essentially a rebel. The dark and elemental passions implicit in him move Philip to go beyond the Blackstable. As Philip feels himself badly in need of succour and sustenance to define and evoke those finer naunces of aesthetic propositions which move him up for freedom. Thwarted and restrained by the conventional ethics of society which is devoid of the mystical and aesthetic manifestations of life. Philip passess through from one predicament to another to search for a foothold for catering to the needs of the 'soul'. All Philip's anguish to find a wayout to his aesthetic and humanistic urges is sneaked with abhorrence. William Carey who stands for the conventional morality ridicules Philip with his apathy. In an identical way Larry's denial to the life of 'happiness' glamour and glory is contrary to the ethics of one and all who opt for nothing but a life of happiness; fun and frolic and above all a materialistic pursuit of life which is taken to be the principal yardstick of attaining success in the modern world.

In Oscar Wilde's 'The Picture of Dorian Gray', beauty sans aesthetic perception, embroils the whole being of man. Dorian to whom beauty comes as a revelation, ironically it to be an end in itself. After undergoing the pain of loneliness, he feels; "He knew that the senses no less than the soul, have their spiritual mysteries to reveal."[10] Maugham dialectically argues that avoidance of pleasure is an act of penance which is in no way an answer to man's search for the spiritual bliss. Maugham like Wilde feels that the role of the 'senses' too could play a pivotal role in innovating a new system in which spiritualization of the senses could cater to the needs of both the body and soul. Dorian Gray after realizing how taking beauty to be a 'sovereign' in itself causes the splitting up of the body and soul. Dorian introspects and realizes that the role of reason too can spiritualize the 'senses'; "He sought to elaborate some new scheme of life that would have its reasoned philosophy and its ordered principles, and find in the spiritualizing of the senses its highest realisation."[11] Maugham too dialectically argues that the violation of the ethics of the soul is tantamount to causing the splitting up of man's personality. He makes defiance of the ethics of the conventional morality which in his opinion is devoid of the aesthetic and spiritual manifestations of life. He dwells upon exploring those areas of darkness which the conventional ethics takes to be an act of abhorrence; a deviation from the mainstream of ethical life. Philip-William relationship basically brings into light the conflict between the conventional ethics and the applied ethics. T. V. Smith throwing light on a variety of volitions writes; "Casuistry—applied ethics—deals with individual moral problems, such as matters of conscience and conflicts of obligation."[12] Maugham like a true exponent of casuistry, points out at those areas of ethical proposition which the conventional ethics is averse to. Hence, it can dialectically be argued that Maugham identifies himself with a casuist who puts up volitions for the expression of those innate aesthetic human propositions in the best possible way. Rebelling against the conventional ethics. Philip like Stephen Dedalus resorts to flight. Stephen Dedalus is pandied to make him fall in line with the established code of morality. Philip too feels his self stifled at king's school when he suffocatingly aspires for escaping to Paris in order to live with the ethics of the soul. Similarly, Larry's escape to Germany awakens in him a new vista of aesthetic perception which takes him off the mainstream of the dictates of the conventional ethics. Strickland escapes to the forlorn of Tahiti in order to discover the domain of truth and freedom evoking the violent and stark savage passions with all their primitiveness in the pictures he paints. Kitty perceives lineaments of hope, reconciliation, spiritual joy and aesthetic beauty in the personage of mother superior who spiritually illustrates that the meaning of real freedom lies neither in man's proclivity to passions nor to living a stoic life instead the real meaning of freedom lies in his retaining the unconquerable spirit of man. Julia suddenly grows conscious of her lack-lustre marriage to Michael who aspires for nothing but money, pelf and power and above all false respectability. Her disillusionment with the 'theatre' of success in which she is put up as a springboard of attaining laurels of success. Like Philip, Larry, and Kitty, Julia too perceives the hypocrisy of the 'real' world in which she is made to enter the 'theatre' of the absurd. Maugham thus projects man-woman relationship and comes to find it devoid of the spiritual and metaphysical vision. Maugham like Shaw regards matrimony as a serious business. Julia humanistically grows conscious of the fallacy of the jarring notes produced by the 'theatre' of success. She aesthetically pines for making herself unattached from the theatrical life of pseudo-success which takes man to utter humiliation and black despair. Her relationship with Tom is however a means to unattach and dismantle herself from the spiritually 'hollow' life of the theatrical personages of the 'real' world. The 'theatre' which Maugham projects on the canvas of his fictional art thus shows how man gets distracted to alienation from the mainstream of life. The relationship which she builds up with Tom, to her is an unavoidable necessity; a means to unattach herself from the cosmetic life of the 'real life' in which every act of performance, every narration and dialogue built up on the stage of theatre, throws man into the ennui and lonelieness Thus her rebellion against the conventional ethics in which money is made to play the role of messiah of success and allurement does nothing but inundate man from within. The sanctity of Maugham's characters thus remains inherent in their endeavour; applied against their bondage to the illusiveness of the 'real life'.

Maugham's characters build up their world in their own image; they struggle against the monstrosity of the mechanical life which tend to seize their soul in their spiritual aberration. Liza Lambeth lacks perspicacity to see the innuendo and malevolence of illusion which ensnare her into the vortex of suffering which has no point of return. Maugham thus invents the need to address the anguish which gets cropped up in the face of the colossal growth of intellect in the mechancial world. Maugham like Yeats is conscious of the existence of the sphinx-like monster which symbolises the emergence of the savage culture, is indifferent to the aesthetic and metaphysical vision. Yeats prefers to remain confined into the cloister of the Ivory Tower cherishing the aesthetic and aristocratic values of life. Yeats is not perturbed at the emergence of the cult of savagery and aspires for living confined into the serenity of the Ivory Tower. Unlike Yeats, Maugham sets syllogistic propositions to evolve a dilectical art to present the cosmic vision by streamlining man, God, and the World. Yeat's erruption of the anguish for the re-integration of the self limits him to the confines of the Ivory Tower. Yeats symbolically writes:

> "Never had I more
> Excited, passionate, fantastical imagination, nor an ear and eye
> That more expected the impossible.
> No, not in boyhood when with rod and fly,
> Or the humbler worm."[13]

The desire to get spiritually purged by the Byzantine saints evokes his idea of the 'beautiful' to behold the revelation of aesthetic and mystical beauty.

Maugham on the other hand moves up out of his Ivory Tower of the Blackstable and aesthetically comes out in the open in the bivouac of life in order to define his stance of emancipation unlike Stephen Dedalus, Philip can't afford to change himself to deal with the horrid situations of the odds of the mechanical life. To Yeats 'ageing' is something akin to a mocking absurdity which compels him to migrate to the city of Byzantium. The anguish of feeling the self threatened in the alien world makes Yeats escape to the city of Byzantium in order to get himself purged at the hands of the Byzantiun saints. Philip in an identical way grapples with the problem of spiritual crisis at the colossal growth of the mechanical society. His escape to Paris is part of a search for freedom from a life of bondage. Larry too like Philip has passion for looking into the Unknown. Larry is well aware of the pitfall of yielding to happiness that makes man too much embroiled at the way the materialistic pursuit of life alienates man from the aesthetic, mystical and metaphysical realizations. Larry does 'nothing' but loiter.

Philip's search for a philosophy which could cater to the needs of art, beauty, clairvoyance and religion—is the basic thrust of his pilgrimage to the denial of happiness. Larry loiters from one place to another to discover and know his self. His refusal to marry Isabel is part of his conviction to make his life aesthetically and metaphysically define at par with his ethical imagination. Maugham looks at the aesthetically alienated life of the modern world through the objective portrayal of characters projected on the canvas of his dialectical art. Maugham's characters are pre-occupied with the zest to look to the outside world in the image whatsoever they are from within. Philip while living at Blackstable feels his life in a trauma. The black despair he undergoes, enkindles in him an orgy of flamboyant emotions to unfetter himself from the onslaught of the mechanical system. Aesthetic sensibility says Somerset Maugham is the basic crux of life which provides man the impetus to translate the canons of the conventional ethics into a concrete reality. Maugham expresses his anguish at the colossal materialistic progress. Man, says Somerset Maugham, ironically runs after the happiness brought about by the mechanics of the modern world. But at the same time, the urge to define his self is equally a palatable force in the alien world. Philip Carey agonisingly looks to the hostile world with a sense of embarrassment. Miss Willkinson yields to her passion giving vent to the outcries of despair, while living in Blackstable. Willkinson's arrival at Blackstable enables Philip to open up a new vista of hope. Philip doesn't believe in the Curater's catholicity in which the diminution of the 'pleasure' braces him up in a state of bondage. Heyward takes the middle path. He on the one had reposes his faith in the church of England believing in 'the whole, the Good and Beautiful' Affirming his faith in the whole of England, Heyward says; "I belong to the Church of England but I love the gold and the silk which clothe the priest of Rome, and his celebacy, and the confessional, and purgatory: and in the darkness of an Italian Cathedral, incense-laden and mysterious, I believe with all my heart in the miracle of the Mass"[14] shows how Maugham takes recourse to putting both the body and soul together to present a complete picture of man where the mind is without the fear of the conventional ethics. Maugham is an artist with a complete vision; firm with the conviction to project life in all its varied shades and designs. Cronshaw remains caught up into the web of dark, primitive and elemental passions projects poetry and becomes pale-faced. He goes all out in adhering to the fury of passion. Living all alone Cronshaw doesn't know the art of adhering to the dynamics of reason to come out of the inclemence of despair. Maugham thus by applying the dialectics of freedom shows a way out how man can unchain and retrieve himself from the tentacles of human bondage. Lawrence's exploration of the instinctual patterns of life is part of his reaction against the drying up of the spiritual and aesthetic vision of life. Like W. B. Yeats Lawrence saw the monstrosity of the mechanical life which he thinks, gave rise to the cessation of the spiritual manifestation of life. Maugham, on the other hand dialectically argues how once the dark savage passions inculcate man into their web, they savagely cut deep down into the being of man pushing him into the throes of pain and black despair. The onslaught of the elemental passions, hence, says Maugham, holds man in a state of bondage. Liza Lambeth in a bid to come out of the trammels of the mundane life, feels herself exilirated to enter into a new life of freedom. Her relationship with Jim Blackeston enhances the intensity of pain and loneliness. Julia in Maugham's 'The Theatre' grows conscious of the hollow and illusive life of the 'Theatre' in which the main thrust is given not on spirituality but on the mere materialistic pursuit of life. She craves for attaining freedom from the cosmetic life of the 'theatre' that could take her to the road to freedom; "She was free of the bondage in which her senses had held her to him and she exulted. Now she could deal with him on equal terms. She stretched out her legs out in bed and sighed with relief."[15] She even goes on to remain indifferent to Roger while breaking away with the bizarre word of the theatre. Neither does she receive respite from her bid of escaping from the tawdry of her theatrical life in her building up relationship with Tom. She too gets aware of Tom's triviality in which the aesthetic emotion had no role to create beauty in her life. Realizing that Tom and Michael are the two faces of the same coin, she scrambles for having herself retrieved from the cosmetic life of the theatre in which she was made to act in the mechanical way. The sudden realization of attaining freedom from the theatrical life, makes her frenzied to come out of the life of spiritual sterility. In his treatment of love and matrimony, the economic factor has been given an umbrage to the aesthetics realization. Disagreeing with Shaw Maugham says that love can not attain transcendence unless it becomes passion. In Maugham's concept of freedom, the meaning of love and marriage has been dealt with a variance. As such the search for freedom, in Shaw's 'candida' begins with Eugene Marchbank's leaving Morel's house with a better secret. All Maugham's characters thus march ahead of the Shavian characters to the road of freedom. Shaw remains irrsolute and undergoes a dlilemma-like situation by employing the art of ambivalence. Unlike Shaw, Maugham takes Shaw's 'real' world to be illusive and unreal taking into account the solipsism which plays a significant role in the making of the self. In "The Enigma of Arrival" V. S. Naipaul exposes the chaotic and directionlessness of the modern world. Hence human life, says Naipaul is riddled with enigma. The 'enigma' of search for emancipation says Naipaul is replete with confusion and intellectual aberration. Naipaul intends to point out at the lack of clarity of the wastelanders who live a spiritually dissipated life. Naipaul's characters never achieve satiety as they go on to argue and caricature endlessly the riddle of the human existence. The 'mutiny' geard up to unfold new horizons of emancipation, ironically inculcates new areas of the 'enigma' of the human existence. Maugham on the other hand probes the enigma of the human existence from the grass-root level emphasizing the need to cultivate a dialectical vision in order to take man to the road of freedom, self-fulfilment, harmony; joy and aesthetic beauty. To Maugham, 'knowledge' is the vehicle of attaining freedom. Experience is thus the key to man's liberation from bondage. Maugham who was immensely influenced by the Indian mythology, unfolds the mystery of liberation. Larry who visits the Indian panorama of the mystical life, feels himself fascinated by the Indian mystics. Larry says; "He sought to wean them away from the slavery of self-hood, passion and sense, and hold them that they could acquire liberation by tranquility, restraint, renunciation, resignation, by steadfastness of mind by an ardent desire for freedom."[16] The cerebral experience Kitty undergoes, makes her cultivate the harvest of tragedy. She no more loves Charles Townsend who is to her is now a trespasser. She feels herself tormented at her getting alienated from the mainstream of life. It is Mother Superior who enkindles in her a new ray of hope which inspires her to come up the life of bondage. Kitty says; "They give up everything, their home, their country, love, children, freedom; and all the little things which I sometimes think must be harder still to give up, flowers and green fields, going for a walk on an autumn day, books and music, comfort, everything they give up, everything. And they do it so that they may devote themselves to a life of sacrifice and poverty, obedience, killing work and prayer. To all of them this world is really and truely a place of exile."[17] Maugham like Lawrence wants to come up every form of bondage that impoverishes man in the mundane world unlike Swift, Maugham is not a pessimist. The humanist in him enkindles hope and courage in order to come out of the tentacles of human bondage. In 'The Painted Veil', Kitty, while living in the alien surroundings feels 'herself' threatened. She agonisingly aspires for freedom; "Freedom! Not only freedom from a bond that irked, and a companionship which depressed her; freedom, not only from the death which had threatened, but freedom from the love that had degraded her; freedom from all spiritual ties, the freedom of a discmbodied spirit; and with freedom, courage and a valiant unconcern for whatever was to come."[18]

With the emergence of the neo-mechanical order, Maugham dialectically searches for new avenues of freedom. The suppression wreaked up by the man-made social constraints, says Maugham, impedes the real growth of emancipation of man. Philip sees hope in making himself rationistically unentwined from the onslaught of passion. Kitty sees redemption in raising herself from every form of bondage. Julia becomes aware of the 'theatre of the absurd' which thrives on the dictum that wants are unlimited. Thus Maugham breaks new ground for the attainment of freedom in which reason, sensitiveness and imagination play a pivotal role in projecting the whole picture of man.

The vortex of loneliness in Larry makes him averse to the cult of the materialistic life. His renunciation of the materialistic life in which money plays a domineering role gives him space for his spiritual revival. Larry is terribly awed at 'the life of the spirits'[19] and evokes spiritual regeneration. He makes Isabel, aware of the mystery of the metaphysics of spirits and says; "I wish I could make you see how exciting the life of spirit is and how rich in experience."[20] Isabel on the other hand is lured into the cult of materialism, has fire and brimstone to enjoy the life of 'Americanism'. For Larry, to yield to a life what Americanism stands for is something akin to "the betrayal of the soul."[21] Isabel who identifies herself with the success-oriented life, ironically lacks aesthetic insight to behold the spiritual and mystical aspects of life. She says; "I don't pretend to be anything but a perfectly normal, ordinary girl. I want to have fun."[22] Isabel rationalistically relates herself with her credo of satisfying her urges—shows how the modern world is inculcated in the cult of the happiness principle. Maugham is a modern existentialist. Like a true existentialist he draws up a line between being and existence. He gives priority and umbrage to the intricacies of experience man passes through. The philosophy of existentialism which emerged against the rational absolutism, argues that man is not purely a rational creature. Instead the basic instincts implicit in him give a new shape to his existence. Hence in Maugham's dynamics of freedom, reason can't be the sole yardstick of probing the mystery of human existence. Paul Roubiczek writes that search for freedom 'should start from one's own experience, one's own knowledge, which should be qualified, enlarged and in this way, enriched.'[23] Mrs. Bradley who looks at the tragectory of Larry, Isabel and Gray Matruin-relationship with objective insight and clarity, undergoes black despair going down deep into the annals of alienation. Mrs. Bradley while having parleys with her brother, Elliott, says; "I'm afraid I've been a sad disappointment to you Elliott, but to tell you the truth I am very satisfied with myself as I am'.[24] Thus the characters Maugham portrays on the dialectical plane, revel in whatever they are from within. Unlike George Orwell, Maugham doesn't project the duality of experience to conceal and maneuver the onslaught of totalitarianism. The ambivalence explored in the Shakespearian drama, conceals the voice of subjectivity. Iago who yields to jeslousy evoking the voice of duality: "I am not what I am."[25] Maugham's characters on the other hand never manoeuvre from the image in which they have been created. Man makes assertion of his 'existence' he experiences. Maugham, with no less sincerity and evocativeness grapples with the problem of human 'existence' which more often than not embroils man in spiritual crisis and vortex of alienation. As such he applies the syllogistic technique to probe the mystery of the human suffering. Maugham unlike, Albert Camus and Jean Paul Satre, stands closer to Kirkegaard and dialectically establishes meaningful relationship between the finite and the infinite. Maugham discards Satre's nothingness and has clairvoyance and insight enough to see meaning, pattern and symphony in the human existence. Life of experience hence, from Maugham's standpoint, becomes a stepping stone to achieve aesthetic and metaphysical joy. Thomas H. Huxley in an identical way, points out at the cosmic processes in which conflict operates between 'existence and experience'. He opines that 'faith born of knowledge', unfolds the metaphysical vision and gives self-fulfilment. Thomas H. Huxley writes; "The faith which is born of knowledge, finds its object in an eternal order, bringing forth ceaseless change, through endless time, in endless space; the manifestation of the cosmic energy attempting between phases of potentiality and phases of explication."[26] It can however be said that Maugham's apocalyptical approach to the human existence is part of his moral vision. The quest for art, beauty and clairvoyance is no less significant than his moral preponderance. Maugham is equally critical of the mechanical society in which man finds himself in the rat race; caught up into the illusive world. Being a disinterested observer Maugham unfolds the mystery of evil with equanimity exploring art, beauty, metaphysics and clairvoyance. From the apocalyptical stand point, Maugham is a terribly religious artist. The 'Pole' in 'The Razor Edge' makes forays into the paradox of evil and says that "the evil is as direct a manifestation of the divine as good. They were strange words to hear in the sordid, noisy cafe, to the accompaniment of dance tunes on the mechanical Piano."[27] Kosti is another character with whom Larry comes across unfolds the mystery of the metaphysical vision explicating how the life of experience becomes a means of linking up the finite and the infinite. Kosti says that he "would talk in a morbid way of the flight from the Alone to the Alone, of the Dark night of the soul and of the final ecstasy in which the creature becomes one with the Beloved."[28] For Maugham beauty alone can't create spiritual and metaphysical elevation unless the element of pleasure is made the moving spectre of beauty. Maugham thus draws a line of demarcation between happiness and 'pleasure'. Dorian Gray in Oscar Wilde's 'The Picture of Dorian Gray' later discovers his self and realizes his self-gratification that makes him alienated from the mainstream of life. To Maugham man's inability to form a balance between ethical and aesthetic aspects of life, gives rise to the endless labyrinth of loneliness. Thus, it is the dichotomy of 'love' and 'passion' in Maugham's fictional world, which causes loneliness, alienation and spiritual embecility in the modern context. In F. H.

Bradley's opinion the self-realization cultivated by virtue of experience retrieves man from the inculcation of human bondage. In Eliot's 'The Waste Land', Tristan-Isolde relationship shows the failure of man-woman relationship and the diminution of domesticity. The Hyacinth girl who is shown entwined into the tentacles, of the worldly and the materialistic life, lacks the perspicacity to perceive the aesthetic and metaphysical dimensions of life. Eliot writes; "You gave me hyacinths a year first ago. They called me the hyacinth girl;"[29]

Somerset Maugham makes the subjective objective by creating a series of human relationship in order to syllogistically probe the metaphysics of love. The characters projected on Maugham's dialectical art, remain conscious of their streams of consciousness which work as the under-currents of the self. Suzanne knows the fallacy and paradox of human relationship in which 'desire' itself can't create harmony and self-fulfilment in the building up of human relationship. Her instincts of ratiocination enables her to realize that her relationship with Larry lacks element of passion which deter her from marrying him. For Maugham, the intermingling of 'love' and 'passion' alone can revive human relationship. The dichotomy of 'love' and 'passion' says Maugham embroils man in the pallor of loneliness and spiritual aberration. Isabel says: "I think it's all stuff and nonesence to say that there can be love without passion...[30]" Maugham thus believes that all the evolutionary and scientific developments without the aesthetic emotion end in a fuss. A true knowledge of the 'self' is the dialectical know how through which Maugham's characters ratiocinate their existence. Suzanne's ability to delve deep into the crux of the problem, liberates her from 'bondage' and spiritual crisis. She says, "My instinct told me I'd be silly to fall in love with him, you know women are very unfortunate, so often when they fall in love they cease to be lovable, and I made up my mind to be on my guard[31]". She comes to realize the objective reality that the metaphysics of love lies ensconsced in the 'loftiness of the soul'. Suzanne says, "She was not silly or mawkish, but she gave one the impression of a lovely purity and a strange loftiness."[32]

Maugham is a disinterested observer of human nature. For him ethics sans aesthetic values leads to the splitting of personality. Susan Stontag rightly says that "every era has to re-invent the project of 'spirituality' for itself (Spirituality = terminologies, ideas of deportment aimed at resolving the painful structural contradictions inherent in human situation, at the completion of consciousness, at transcendence)".[33] The new myth says Somerset Maugham derives its impetus from the post psychological conception of consciousness, exists within the activity of art. Stontag delineates art's relation to consciousness says that in "the early linear version of art's relation to consciousness, a struggle was discovered between the 'spiritual' integrity of the creative impulses and the distracting 'materiality' of ordinary life".[34] Throwing light on 'Arts' for 'Art' sake, he discuses at length the perception regarding art's relation to consciousness. Firstly the myth is treated as "an expression of human consciousness seeking to know itself'.[35] On the other hand the later version of the myth denies that art is mere expression. The "Later myth, says Stontag, rather relates art to the mind's need or capacity for self estrangement. Art is no longer understood as conscious expressing and therefore, implicitly affirming itself. Art is not consciousness per se, but rather its antidote—evolved from within consciousness itself."[36] Stontag thus identifies "the newer version, in which art is part of a dialectical transaction with consciousness, poses a deeper more frustrating conflict. The 'spirit' seeking embodiment in art clashes with the material character of art itself .[37] Maugham on the other hand belongs to the later version of Myth according to which art is not a mere expression instead, it opens areas of self-estrangement leading his character to achieve freedom on the dialectical plane. Forster too like Maugham, too takes the solipsistic technique to be a vehicle of projecting 'order' in the true sense. The classicists like Alexander Pope define order in terms of form and decorum that give out artistic finish. Both Maugham and Forster concentrate on the doctrine of the inner self which alone, to them, could produce 'order' in the true sense. Forster writes; "Order I suggest is something evolved from within nor something imposed from without; it is an internal stability or a vital harmony and in the social and political category it has never existed except for the convenience of distortions".[38] D. H. Lawrence emphasizes to shed the 'old skin' Forster in a identical way. Prophecies the decay of the hollowness of the 'real' world. Forster writes; "The Human race has never undergone it, and is still too perky to admit that it may be coming and might result in a sprouting of new growth through the decay."[39] J. W. N. Sullivan in this regard rightly says that "science is not created by the scientific outlook; it is scientific knowledge that creates the outlook".[40] Elaborating the limitations of science, Sullivan further says 'that' the science of Physics is concerned only with those aspects of the world which can be treated in the qualitative terms. Sullivan like Maugham too believes that "science itself does not assume that it alone is concerned with the real. The statements of science are true within the limited region it claims for itself—the region of mathematical structure."[41] Maugham who is well-conscious of the ambiguities of the collocations of atoms, dialectically says that the science of new Physics and a knowledge of mathematical structure can too open up a new vista of metaphysical realizations. Bertrand Russell who is critical of the materialistic outlook also says that "man is the product of causes which had no provision of the end they were achieving; that his origin, his growth, his hopes and fears, his loves and beliefs, are but the outcome of accidental collocations of atoms;"[42] Bertrand Russell says that the "good life is one inspired by love and guided by knowledge."[43] Maugham on the one hand regards the metaphysics of love as a liberating factor for the homo sapiens in the modern age. Bertrand Russell, elaborating the meaning of the 'good life' says; "When I said that the good life consists of love guided by knowledge, the desire which prompted me was the desire to live such a life as far as possible, and to see others living it; and the logical content of the statement is that, in a community where men live in this way, more desires will be satisfied than in one where there is less love or less knowledge."[44] The good life says Russell, emanates from love coupled with knowledge. In Maugham's dynamics of freedom, love can't achieve transcendence unless it is made to exist with passion. For Maugham, the basic instincts implicit in man evokes a new being which is beyond the purview of the "the scientific objective knowledge"[45] Hence, in order to present the whole being of man, the basic instincts, says Karl Jaspers, need to be taken into account as the 'real' and the psycho-analytical study of probing the whole and the cumulative being of man. Pointing out at the limitations of science Karl Jaspers writes; "Scientific objective knowledge is not knowledge of being. This means that scientific knowledge is particular not general, that it is directed toward specific objects and not onward Being itself."[46] Karl Jaspers does not take human freedom to be an "object of science"[47] instead to him, it is "the field of philosophy. Within the purview of science there is no such thing as liberty."[48] T. H. Huxley takes into account the "faith, which is born of knowledge,"[49] the crucial factor in breaking a new ground, a new ethics which in his opinion, gives an added dimension to the being of man. To Karl Jaspers, scientific objective knowledge is indefferent to both 'the beautiful' and 'the ugly'. Karl Jaspers writes; "The new urge for knowledge sees the World no longer as simply beautiful. This knowledge ignores the beautiful and the ugly, the good and the wicked."[50] Jaspers thus establishes art's relation between freedom and communication. It is man's freedom which enables him to communicate to the real world. Freedom, as such Jaspers says, doesn't exist in isolation instead freedom communicates to the real world, is the basics through which man achieves transcendence. Maugham like Karl Jaspers thus believes that transcendence is not his freedom; instead it lies in the exercise of freedom. Karl Jaspers further writes; "My reality lies in my freedom which is tantamount to imperfectability. I am free in the necessity—I feel as guilt. But this reality lies already in its own transcendence. Transcendence is not my freedom, but it is in my freedom."[51] Paul Roubiczek, too believes that the solipsistic and subjective art alone can probe and deal with the scientific knowledge in order to carve out a balance between the ideal and the real. Such quantitative interpretation of the scientific facts says Sullivan ignores the aesthetic and metaphysical aspects of human life. Karl Jaspers in his concept of freedom, philosophically argues that the new urge for the pursuit of knowledge ignores the ugly and the beautiful making man embroil in the endless labyrinth of loneliness.

Love, in Sarojini Naidu's realm of freedom, plays a purificatory role making man metaphysically and mystically conscious enough to come up the dross of the earthly and the mundane experiences. 'Pain' says Sarojini Naidu makes man undergo the cathartic and the condescending process making man spiritually purged. Philip in Maugham's 'Of Human Bondage' undergoes the intensity of the savage emotions which cut him from within. Sarojini Naidu writes :

> "And love shall burn thee like a fire,
> And pain shall cleanse thee like a flame,
> To purge the dross from thy desire."[52]

Walter Pater too aesthetically believes that pleasure is the sole purpose of art. To him art no longer should play a subservient role in depicting the complete picture of man. Croce categorically defines reality into two—one existing in the mind and other outside the mind. Similarly he categorises knowledge into two types—one is intuitive which is obtained through imagination whereas the other form of knowledge pertains to individual things. Croce gives shape to impressions which he says makes indelible imprint into the human psyche. Art says Croce is a vehicle of intuition or the expression of an impression within the substance of mind. It enables the mind to receive millions of impulses and arrives at certain conclusions. Having received the tint of imagination those impressions which remain implicit become evocatively explicit. Thus in Maugham's depiction of dialectical art, the assertion of faith becomes explicit and 'visible'—is one of the striking features of Maugham's art and morality. Maugham's exploration of 'passion' on the dialectical plane, is not mere perfunctory instead, the moral and ethical vision lie ensconced -with the aesthetic sensibility. Maugham writes; "unless love is passion, it isn't true, but something else; and passion thrives not on satisfaction but on impediment."[53] Yeats is identically conscious of the fury of passion that persists as a driving force in him. Like Maugham Yeats elevates himself from the subjective to the objective plane by defining love as a palatable force. As Maud Gonne emerges in every poetic line Yeats writes, makes himself unable to detach the magic, she casts upon him. As such Yeats aesthetically explicates the metaphysics of love and intends to know:

> "Does the imagination dwell the most
> Upon a woman won or woman lost ?"[54]

Maugham thus applies a phycho-analytical study of the substance of the human mind, as to him the deep seated passion has a being of its own giving a new shape to the human consciousness Maugham who is mystically aware of the palatable power of the passion, writes; "It destroyed Antony and Cleopatra, Tristan and Isolde, Parnell and Kitty O' Shea. And if it doesn't destroy it dies."[55] Like Sarojini Naidu, Maugham dialectically argues that 'pain' is a vehicle by virtue of which man passes through the purifictory processes and becomes spiritually purged. The onslaught of pain is thus part of the cathartic process which makes man undergo the emotions of pity and fear and comes to realize that the mind, soul and the body constitute the whole of the human existence. Yeats too probes the human existence and finds out organic unity in every iota of the human existence. Yeats poetically writes;

"O chestnut-tree, great-rooted blossomer,
Are you the leaf, the blossom or the bole ?
O body swayed to music, O brightening glance,
How can we know the dancer from the dance ?[56]

Maugham's search for freedom operates on the ethical, aesthetic, moral, artistic and apocalyptical planes. He shows his anguish at Man's running after the spiritually lack lustre illusive life. He aesthetically finds man caught up into the labyrinth of dilemma and illusion. The schism between the ingrained consciousness and the illusive life Man runs after, creates the cobweb of man's spiritual alienation. Maugham unlike the socialistic writers like W.H. Auden and Stephen Spender, doesn't take the social hierarchy in terms of the economic maladjustment operating between 'haves' and 'havenots'; instead he is a writer who looks at the suffering humanity not from the economic stand point but from the aesthetic aspect. The human bondage persisting in the modern era, says Maugham is a byproduct of the discord between consciousness and his illusive life. Maugham is neither perturbed at the squalor, poverty and slum-dwelling nor bewildered at the endless urbanization. For him the prevalence of squalor, poverty and economic deprivation is itself a part of the human consciousness. Maugham comes to perceive the whole panorama of man only in co-relating the prevalence of squalor, poverty with the Infinite. He comes to perceive the 'beautiful' after he realizes that the real beauty emerges in human life in taking them to be part of the human consciousness. Shaw, Wells and Galsworthy who had expressed their anguish and concern at the social injustices which economically corroded human being not from within but from without. Orwell takes human bondage in terms of cessation of individual integrity. Human bondage says Orwell remains hidden 'inside the whale' of the totalitarian powers; the twin orthodoxies of the socialistic and capitalistic systems that subdue the spirit of man. Graham Greene evokes the ministry of fear by the vehicle of the catholic dogma. Maugham on the other hand starts the journey of discovering the realm of truth and freedom from the consciousness itself. Maugham thus establishes relation between art and consciousness; he comes to realize that the cult of realism is no more relevant to explore the dialectical consciousness; the consciousness which provides feed back to both to the scientific and aesthetic aspects of life. Man's falling prey to impulse, says Maugham is itself another dimension of human bondage. The instinct implicit in man itself invents reasons to seek manifestation in externalities of human behaviour.

Somerset Maugham's novels are a vivid spectrum of exploring the humanistic urges of attaining freedom from the painted veil of the 'real' world. Maugham is a disillusioned realist who emphasizes the need to explore the ingrained motley colours of the self. Maugham therefore is of the view that the realistic cult of writing no more plays a significant role in streamlining the aesthetic emotion with the colossal upsurge of intellect. Maugham writes;

"I sighed for the liberty of fiction and thought with pleasure of the lonely reader who was willing to listen to all I had to say and without whom I could effect intimacy that I could never hope for in the garish publicity of the theatre"[57]. Maugham who was deeply influenced by Spinoza's concept of 'self-realization' which in his opinion opens up a new horizon of emancipating Man from the life of frivolity and bondage persisting in the real world. In Maugham's dynamics of freedom, 'consciousness' is inter-related with self-realization. The search for freedom in Maugham's realm of freedom begins with a sudden awareness of the consciousness from within. The consciousness enkindled in Man acts as an instrument to define his stance of life in the painted world of the 'senses' and 'illusion' which ultimately create the way for self-realization. Thus, the inbuilt basics of consciousness on which Maugham's portrayal of Man takes place, emancipates him from bondage. Maugham writes; "We may suppose that consciousness was enkindled in Man as an instrument to enable him to deal with his environment and that for long ages it reached too higher development that was needed to deal with the vital problems of his practice."[58] In Of Human Bondage, Man has been shown dangling in despair in the face of the colossal upsurge of intellect. Philip jumbles from one predicament to another in order to search for a foothold in a society that could cater to his aesthetic emotion. Philip-Mildred relationship can be regarded as man's frantic search for emancipation in the modern society. Larry in The Razor's Edge revels in the 'self-sacrifice'. Being averse to the American cult of the happiness principle he wants to do 'nothing'. To Larry, to opt for the materialistic pursuit of happiness is to deny the 'consciousness' which is essential for 'the survival of the individual'. In 'The summing up' Maugham says that "there is a singular delight in self-sacrifice few would deny, and in so far as it offers a new field for activity and the opportunity to develop a new side of the self, it has value in self-realization".[59] Larry's denial to marry Isabel is part of the aesthetic perception that enables him to search for a 'new' fodder for catering to his consciousness. Maugham was a great admirer of Goethe who intrinsically held self-realization to be a stepping stone of attaining the physical realities of life. Showing immense admiration for Goethe, Maugham writes; "Aristotle has said that the end of human activity is right action, and Goethe that the secret of life is living. I suppose that Goethe means that man makes the most life when he arrives at self realization"[60]

In 'The Razor's Edge,' 'desire' says Maugham is devoid of the metaphysical dimension. Differentiating 'desire' from passion, Maugham, writes; "Of course there can be desire without love. Desire isn't passion. Desire is the natural consequence of the sexual instinct and it isn't of any more importance than any other function of the human animal."[61] In Maugham's metaphysics, Love can't achieve transcendence "Unless love is passion, it is not love, but something else; and passion thrives not on satisfaction but on impediment".[62] The fury of passion Philip and Larry undergo makes them rebel against the prevalence of the conventional ethics. The world cropped up by the colossal growth of scientific facts hardly offers them any space to cater to their aesthetic aspirations. Unlike Larry Isabel opines that "the best way to overcome desire is to satisfy it".[63] Maugham, in the face of feeling his self, threatened in the alien world, scrambles for freedom from the state of bondage. He applies the dialectical art to probe and see how the dark savage passions hold man in a state of bondage emphasizing that the 'senses' too can cleanse the soul. The experience cropped up by the evolutionary and scientific developments, leads man to loneliness and bondage. The pain of loneliness, says Maugham, thus enkindles in man an urge to rationalistically know the limitations of the 'real' world. Maugham writes; "and it is only by degrees, through pain, that he understands the fact of the body. And experiences of the same kind are necessary for the individual to become conscious of himself; but here there is the difference that, although everyone becomes equally conscious of his body as a separate and complete organism, everyone doest not become equally conscious of himself as a complete and separate personality".[64] Thus experience is an instrument through which the individual becomes conscious of the mettle of the self. In 'Of Human Bondage' Maugham aesthetically explores how the 'spirit' implicit in man aspires for freeing "itself from the bonds of the flesh and he seemed to be living a new life".[65] Philip feels the fury of the spirit realizing how all the evolutionary and scientific jargons inculcated in the modern era, are part of the illusion that makes Man undergo spiritual emptiness, alienation and loneliness. The pain of loneliness thus awakens him to the world of spirit and above all to freedom from bondage. Wharton, to whom Philip gets accustomed during his sojourn in Germany, philosophically bifurcates freedom into two—"freedom of thought and freedom of action"[66]. Wharton explains how the meaning of freedom varies from country to country; Wharton is overwhelmed with the worst kind of freedom which he sees in England where freedom of thought can't be translated into freedom of action; "But in England you get neither: you're ground down by convention. You can't think as you like and you can't act as you like."[67] Feeling himself threatened and stifled into the confines of Blackstable, Philip too like Wharton feels himself alien in his own surroundings. The aesthetic emotion implicit in him itself invents reasons to define the self. The rebel in Philip, thus passes through one predicament to another to find aesthetic foothold for survival of the 'individual' he is. He would not yield to the conventional ethics which he feels impinched upon himself from the outside; "Faith had been forced upon him from the outside. It was a matter of environment and example. A new environment and new example gave him the opportunity to find himself. He put off the faith of his childhood quite simply, like a cloak that he no longer needed."[68] The prevalence of the 'real' life says Maugham is something akin to eluding to self illusory life. To see things, as they are perceived by the beholder, to him, is to yield to illusion, Eliot, on the one hand exposes the skull beneath the skin. For him sordid realities of the modern life, have been realistically regarded as a 'heap of broken images'. Maugham applies the technique of the paradox according to which the 'real' becomes 'unreal'; the invisible visible. Maugham aesthetically writes,

> "It is an illusion that youth is happy, an illusion of those who have lost it; but the young know they are wretched, for they are full of the truthless, ideals which have been instilled into them and each time they come in contact with the real they are bruised and wounded. It looks as if they were victims of a conspiracy; for the books they read, ideal by the necessity of selection, and the conversation of their elders, who look back upon the past through a rosy haze of forgetfulness, prepare them for an unreal life."[69]

In his exposition of the 'real' world, Maugham rationalistically says that the more is the fulfilment of the desire the more is the degree of disappointment and dissatisfaction in their 'Wasteland'; All their materialistic pursuit of life they hanker after, becomes an impediment to elevation of the soul. The denizens of the real world, to their horror, find themselves a prisoner of their self illusory-life. Maugham writes; "They must discover for themselves that all they have read and all they have been told are lies, lies, lies; and each discovery is another nail driven into the body on the cross of life. The strange thing is that each one who has gone through that bitter disillusionment adds to it in his turn, unconsciously, by the power within him which is stronger than himself."[70] In Orwell's search for freedom, the vehicle of double speak is exercised to conceal the inherent consciousness. All the mundane and sordid realities that exist in the outside world enkindle in Philip an urge; a consciousness to see the finite things as they are. With the realization that finite objects are part of the whole human consciousness, Philip is no more averse to them; He "clamoured for life as it stood; sordidness, vice, deformity, did not offend him; he declared that he wanted man in his nakedness; and he rubbed his hands when an instance came before him of meanness, cruelty, selfishness, or lust: that was the real thing."[71] In Paris, Philip comes to realize that there was neither ugliness nor beauty instead both the ugliness and beauty constitute the whole truth and human consciousness. He comes to gather the impression that realism is no more an answer for wiping out the ills of the society prevailing in the post modern era. Maugham rather feels himself more inclined to "the inward life might be as manifold, as varied, as rich with experience, as the life of one who conquered realms and explored unknown lands."[72] In 'Of Human Bondage', Maugham searches for a greater reality that could cater to man's aesthetic sense. For Shaw, a life of romance and idealism was of no consequence. In 'Candida' Morel's metaphors and his speeches made to the large audience, don't address man's inward search for emancipation. For Maugham the search for beauty devoid of the aesthetic and the inward life; is merely sentimental and illusive. Maugham thus dialectically argues that the realistic cult of writing is no more feasible for projecting the fuller perspective of man in the modern era. Philip feels; "He felt vaguely that here was something better than realism which he had adored;"[73]. Shaw was aghast at the squalor and dungeons of poverty. He was an anti-romantic playwright in the sense that he saw that all the ills of society—poverty, slum dwelling, prostitution, War and pseudo-democracy are all a byproduct of economic deprivation. He was an iconoclast in the sense that he believes in breaking the high ideals of romanticism and its philosophy of escaping from the sordid and the mundane world. Wells dreamt of transforming the society into a scientific utopia. Shaw was averse to poverty squalor and other sordid realities. Maugham unlike Wells and Shaw on the other hand, dialectically accepts ugliness beauty squalor taking them to be a part of the whole human consciousness and a stepping stone of beholding into the unknown. Realizing the inadequacies of the cult of realism, Maugham writes; "but certainly it was not the bloodless idealism which accepted aside from life in weakness; it was too strong; it was virile; it accepted life in all its vivacity ugliness and beauty, squalor and heroism; but it was realism still; but it was realism carried to some higher pitch, in which facts were transformed by the more vivid light in which they were seen."[74]

Maugham unlike Shaw is a disillusioned realist. What Maugham is basically concerned is to retrieve man from the illusiveness of the 'real' world which to him causes the onslaught of alienation, rootlessness, discord and the dissipation of the flesh and spirit. Therefore, experience is the instrument says Maugham, which can play a dialectical role in dismantling the illusive life of the spiritually hollow Modern Wasteland.

References

1. Anthony curtis; p. 70.
2. Thomes H. Huxley, Evolution and ethics: and other essays", Macmillan and co., Limited, st. Martin's street, London, ed., 1925, p. 8.
3. Oscar Wilde; The picture of Dorian Gray, p. 35.
4. Somerset Maugham; The Razor's Edge, p. 386.
5. Ibid., p. 368.
6. William Shakespeare; King Lear, The Complete Works, p. 1074.
7. T.S. Eliot; Selected Poems, p. 67.
8. Oscar Wilde; p. 109.
9. *Op.cit.*
10. *Op.cit.*
11. Oscar Wilde; The Picture of Dorian Gray, p. 181.
12. E.M. Albert; T.C. Denise, S.P. Peter Freund; Great Tradition in Ethics, Eurasia Publishing House (P.) Ltd., New Delhi, ed., 1968, p. 4.
13. W.B. Yeats; Tower, selected poetry, edited by A. Norman Jeffares, p. 105.
14. W. Somerset Maugham; Of Human Bondage, p. 132.
15. W. Somerset Maugham; The Theatre Heinemann/Octopus/ Martin Seeker and Warburg, London, ed. 1979, p. 577.
16. W. Somerset Maugham; The Razor's Edge, p. 514.
17. W. Somerset Maugham; The Painted Veil, p. 191.
18. *Ibid.*, p. 205.

19. W. Somerset Maugham; The Razor's Edge, p. 386.
20. *Ibid.*
21. *Ibid.*
22. *Ibid.*, p. 396.
23. Quoted by Paul Roubiczek: Existentialism For and Against, London; Cambridge University Press, ed., 1964, p. 10.
24. W. Somerset Maugham; The Razor's Edge, p. 389.
25. *Op.cit.*
26. Thomas H. Huxley; Evolution and Ethics, Macmillan and Co. Limited, London, ed., 1925, p. 8.
27. W. Somerset Maugham; The Razor's Edge, p. 406.
28. *Ibid.*, p. 407.
29. T.S. Eliot; The Wasteland, Selected Poems, p. 52.
30. W. Somerset Maugham; The Razor's Edge, p. 445.
31. *Ibid.*, p. 457.
32. *Ibid.*, p. 465.
33. Susan Stontag; The Aesthetics of silence, edited by William J. Handy and Max Westbrook, Light and Life Publishers, ed., 1974, p. 453.
34. *Ibid.*, p. 454.
35. *Ibid.*, pp. 453-454.
36. *Ibid.*
37. *Ibid.*
38. E.M. Forster; 'Art for Art sake', The Conscious Reader, Caroline Shrade/Harry Fine Stone, p. 432.
39. *Ibid.*, p. 433.
40. J.W.N. Sullivan; The Limitations of science, A Mentor book published by the New American Library, ed., 1963, p. 8.
41. Ibid., p. 162.
42. Quoted by. J.W.N. Sullivan, Limitations of Science, p. 133.
43. Bertrand Russell; 'What I believe', Why I am not a Christian and other essays on religion and related subjects, edited by Paul Edwards, George Allen and Unwin Ltd., London, ed., 1964, p. 44.
44. Bertrand Russell; What I believe, p. 49.
45. Karl Jaspers; "Is science evil," The conscious Reader, Caroline Shrades, Macmillan Publishing Co., Inc., New York, ed., 1974, p. 728.

46. *Ibid.*
47. *Ibid.*
48. *Ibid.*, p. 728.
49. *Op.cit.*
50. *Ibid.*, p. 729.
51. Quoted by Roshan Ara; 'Jasper's Concept of Freedom', The Aligarh Magazine, Aligarh Muslim University, Aligarh, ed., 1979, p. 80.
52. Sarojini Naidu; Indian English Poetry, Orient Longman, Patna, ed., 1997, p. 24.
53. W. Somerset Maugham; The Razor's Edge, p. 446.
54. W.B. Yeats; Selected Poetry, Radha Publishing House, Calcutta, p. 109.
55. W. Somerset Maugham; The Razor's Edge, p. 446.
56. W.B. Yeats. Selected Poetry; Among School Children, p. 130.
57. W. Somerset Maugham, The Summing Up, p. 114
58. *Ibid.*, p. 206
59. *Ibid.*, p. 207
60. *Ibid.*, pp. 206-207
61. W. Somerset Maugham., The Razor's Edge, p. 446.
62. *Ibid.*
63. *Ibid.*
64. W. Somerset Maugham, Of Human Bondage, p. 54.
65. *Ibid.*, p. 81.
66. *Ibid.*, p. 113.
67. *Ibid.*
68. *Ibid.*, p. 139.
69. *Ibid.*, p. 144.
70. *Ibid.*
71. *Ibid.*, p. 544.
72. *Ibid.*, p. 545.
73. *Ibid.*
74. *Ibid.*

8
Post Script

Dialectics of freedom in Maugham's art and literature is an intermingling of the scientific, moral and aesthetic experiences of life that project emancipation from the inclemence of human bondage. Maugham while defining the innate and manifold humanistic dimensions of human nature, emphasizes the evocativeness of the human spirit. Man says Somerset Maugham has always been quizzically looking up for the areas in which he could define the self in the multi-ethnic and multicultural society. Passing through the ordeal of the cathartic processes, he feels himself, purged of the dehumanization caused by the colossal growth and inculcation of the scientific developments. The transcendence he achieves by undergoing the aesthetic emotion, becomes a stepping stone of dismantling the pain of loneliness. The business of life is thus a pilgrimage; an incessant search for spiritual bliss and self-fulfilment on the dialectical plane. The interplay of the scientific, ethical and aesthetic aspects becomes transmuted into one organic and cumulative experience. The implicit dialectical perspective alone can unfold the riddle of the human existence. It can however be said that man's undergoing a state of experience is an unavoidable necessity for the aesthetic and spiritual realizations. The whole business of human life is thus a pilgrimage; an incessant search for a life of transcendence and self-fulfilment on the dialectical plane. Larry in Maugham's 'The Razor's Edge', does 'nothing' but 'loaf'. Getting aware of the aesthetic upsurge in him, he paints wintry landscapes. Being hit by the onslaught of loneliness, he makes inquisition and defines his 'self' in the bizarre outside world in order to cater to his self-fulfilment. Philip's frantic search for a foothold; his escape to Paris to see his career in painting and his enthusiastic discourse to Heyward, Cronshaw, Fanny Price and even with Mildred, is part of his search for a way out to the anguish that he undergoes. Maugham's characters lookup to the outside world to opt for a way of life catering to the ethics and aesthetics of their throbbing self. His characters never look back and get bedeviled at their plight; they look stranger to the bizarre world and feel febrile and fervid with the hope of unfolding new horizons of emancipation. In George Orwell's dynamics of human relationship, the protagonists surreptitiously make all out efforts to conceal their identity behind the 'painted veil' of the double speak in order to get divulged from the nightmare of totalitarianism. It is the objective feeling hidden beneath the 'veil' of double speak which matters most to the Orwellian protagonist. The act of concealment is put up on the 'painted veil' to cover up their identity in Maugham's exploration of emancipation. Nor does man in his search of freedom know the art of employing the vehicle of the double speak, instead, they eclectically get evocative in their bid to define the trauma of self. In 'The Theatre' of success and false respectability, Julia passes through her hallucinatory experiences after getting aware of her spiritually aberrated life. She is made to realize how she is nothing but a plaything in her theatrical performances. The life of physicality explained in terms of her theatrical performances makes her aesthetically awakened to a new being. She feels herself no different from Phoenix; something akin to a new woman born of the 'knowledge' of her own physicality. Larry in an identical way, undergoes a change of heart. The disastrous war he himself sees with his own eyes, brings about a total transformation making his mantle a new being. Kitty was oblivious of herself before giving assent for marrying Walter. The realization that she is a cog in the wheel of the theatrical establishments, Julia gets alienated to and aspires for freedom from the void which was lingering over. Her growing relationship with Tom is part of her volition to get away from the satraps of her marital discord. But in no time does she realize how Michael and Tom symbolically emerge as trespassers to the integrity of human relationships. She regains her freedom in re-integrating the human spirit. For Maugham real meaning and applicability of freedom exist in Man's dialectically believing in the inviolableness of the human spirit. In Maugham's dialectical art, the soul has a propensity to define itself in every stance man takes in the face of dealing with the trials and tribulations of the earthly and the mundane life. The cataclysmic change taking place in Maugham's characters muster up reason enough not to be lured into the business and paraphernalia of the earthly and the mundane life. The life of experience in Maugham's dynamics of freedom takes man to the attainment of the life of purgation and transcendence. Empiricism is thus the beginning of man's initial perception of an object or of a view which in turn takes man to his adherence to knowledge. Thus difference between empiricism and knowledge lies only in the degree. Keeping in view of his passing through the temporary phases of empiricism; man just draws outlines of reasoning in which he builds up his dialectical perception. Bertrand Russell in an identical way, is conscious of the basic instincts which give a new shape to the making of the human existence. Both Russell and Maugham dialectically define the extent to which the scientific collocations of atoms would be extended, should be such that they shouldn't abjure the 'instinct'. Russell rationalistically writes; "Instinct has its rights and if we do violence to it beyond a point it takes vengeance in subtle ways. Therefore in aiming at a good life the limits of human possibility must be borne in mind. Here again, however, we are brought back to necessity of knowledge"[1]

The enkindling of the aesthetic awareness in man paves the way for a new threshold of freedom in which the soul basks in glory; enthused and conscious of the elements which constitute the being and existence of man. Larry after undergoing the devastating experience of the war, comes to realise that everything that glitters is not aesthetically 'beautiful'. Maugham thus applies syllogistic technique to probe the intricacies of life. The dialectical art thus says Maugham can define the 'beautiful' and the awesomeness of the human spirits man aspires for. Unlike Larry and Philip, Gray Matruin who is a by-product of the materialistic pursuit of life, ironically equates life in terms of premium. Similarly the mechanical life Michael hankers after is ironically to be realised in terms of the laurels of success through his theatrical establishments. Maugham's characters thus move up with the idea of the 'beautiful' which gives them the power of differentiating between the sacred and the profane.

Maugham like T.S. Eliot, is too conscious of the negative impact of the scientific facts that besmear and bemuse man in the modern world. In Maugham's dialectics of freedom, the real crux of ordeal begins with the empirical reasoning of the the crises he comes across. The process of ratiocination passes through the various phases of empiricism, knowledge and experience, enabling man for a better understanding of the 'self' and the 'real' world. It shows how the ordeal of attaining freedom on the dialectical plane, proceeds in the linear direction. Thus, empiricism, accumulation of knowledge and experience are the pre-requisites of the aesthetic, spiritual and the metaphysical aspects of life. It can however be dialectically argued that the aesthetic and metaphysical dimensions of human life, are a condominium over the songs of experience. The scientific developments, provide a vehicle of generating hope instilling the 'faith' which is born of the scientific and mechanical developments, don't stifle the self; instead the rationalistic propensity ensconced with the ethical and aesthetic realizations, open up are new dawn of hope and redemption to man in the post modern civilization. Thus Maugham's concept of transcendence lies not in freedom instead it lies in the exercise of freedom itself. The pilgrims' progress which basically begins from the empirical perception, takes man to the joy of the aesthetic beauty. In 'The Prelude' William Wordsworth laments at his inability to communicate with Nature. Retreating to the landscape of Nature, Wordsworth unveils the mystical revelation of beauty. In Maugham's landscape of freedom, man on the dialectical plane, eclectically enters the domain of varied experiences. Bearing the burden of loneliness he yearns for perceiving the unperceivable. Larry loiters into the dark and frantically searches for the scafolding of the ways of means to define his self in consonance with the inertia of the self he has within. Philip paints desolatory landscapes in a bid to dialectically know the delicate naunces of the metaphysics of love. To Maughm thus yielding to basic instincts, causes the real crux of human bondage. Getting unentwined from the tentacles of the internecine bondage to passion, to him, means for real freedom to be realised on the dialectical plane. In Eliot's, The Waste Land the nature of love explored by the portrayal of Tristan-lslode relationship shows that love in thc modern age has undergone a sea-change. Maugham hence dialectically points out at the change in the human perception that has dismantled the pre-industrial society. With the realization that the collocation of atoms has given rise to a new set of human values in the post modern society, Maugham emphasizes the need to spiritualise the senses in order to be at par with his ethics and aesthetics. Maugham thus syllogistically interminges the psychic, ethical and aesthetic elements into a dialectical whole.

Truth says Somerset Maugham doesn't manifest itself without the idea of the 'beautiful'. Mahatma Gandhi, on the other hand, Philosophically says that freedom can't be achieved both on the physical and the mystical planes unless it becomes a concrete reality. Thus in the Gandhian realm of freedom, 'truth' is the prerogative of beauty which alone can take man to his road to freedom. Gandhi begins his pilgrimage of freedom from the truth itself. So staunch was his faith in the dynamics of the truth that nothing could divulge him from realising the dream of emancipation by the yardstick of the truth. In the Gandhian domain of freedom beauty assumes a secondary role for championing the cause of the truth. Beauty says John Keats, Sans truth, is a partial revelation of a work of art. In Maugham's dialectics of freedom, truth and beauty, art and morality and above all ethics and aesthetics constitute the genesis of the 'beautiful'. Truth from the aesthetic standpoint, says Maugham, is as significant as the ethical imagination which lies deeply interwoven into the fabric of a work of art. Orwell stresses the need to perform a balance between the 'yogi' and the 'commissar'. His insistence on a balanced human relationship is the basic crux on which he pins his hope of retrieving man from the onslaught of totalitarianism. Maugham on the other hand, concentrates on the inertia of the self in order to thwart and restrain the pain of loneliness. With the realisation that human spirit can't be put up barricaded for long, Julia in Maugham's 'The Theatre' feels herself frenzied and enraptured to sing her song of freedom. Looking back at her life of bondage, she had had to live suffocatively, she goes on to the extent of impulsively yielding to Tom. Maugham's characters search for new horizons of freedom wherein they could find a better pasture for defining their self in a world which is essentially mechanical. Unlike the Romantics, Maugham is not an escapist nor a realist the way Shaw is, instead he is an artist with a dialectical vision taking life the way it manifests itself to man. The key to achieving transcendence and spiritual elevation, as such, lies not in freedom but in the exercise of freedom; a new dawn of freedom and transcendence can be dialectically realized in man's essentially retaining his spirits. The wages of unreason entwines Fanny price into the untold miseries of life. Philip too in an identical way doesn't know how to retrieve himself from the onslaught of passion which seizes his soul up in frenzy, thus, Maughm's approach to life rationalises the dark and elemental passions giving man a new thrill of aesthentic perception.

Maugham's dialectical approach rationalises the innate and dark savage passions which tend to define themselves in every throb of human life. The cult of happiness no more remains the sole pursuit of happiness. Man then no more identifies himself with a society in which the whole business of life runs after the materialistic pursuit of life. Being caught up into the web of the savage passions. Man says Maugham, finds himself inculcated into a state of human bondage. The tentacles of human bondage as such, are directly related with man's search for emancipation. Maugham thus brings into focus those forms of human bondage that persist in society. Maugham ardently argues that the human endeavour and his dream of attaining freedom would remain incomplete unless man evolves a dialectical know how; a rationalistic faculty to identify various forms of human bondage. It is this implied dialectical approach says Maugham which enables man to reason and identify various facets of human bondage. What Maugham's dialectical art intends to know is to make man aware of the illusion of happiness that pushes him into the throes of loneliness. His characters never look back and make compromises with their stance of life. Maugham's dialectical art thus opens up a third dimension giving space to those basic instincts which evocatively get manifest in the behavioural patterns of the post modern society. Thus the innate and the dark passions enkindle in man a new beacon of hope and resuscitation of spirits opening up a new domain of freedom wherein Man is no more threatened by the illusive life of the 'real' world. Maugham however basically argues how the modern world with all its colossal scientific and technological developments ironically fails to retrieve man from human bondage. Maugham's dialectical approach thus rationalises all the human endeavour applied to the evolutionary, scientific and technological planes in order to place man in the correct perspective.

The dialectical art interwoven into the texture of Maugham's writings—novels, stories and essays, intend to explore various nuances of art and literature. The dialectical art he carves out, thus forms a counterpoise between ethics and aesthetics. Maugham never divulges from making assertion of the moral tone and tenor that essentially emanate from his writings. The exquisite beauty, art and the clairvoyance which he intermingles in his dialectical art create artistic elevation enabling man to come up the colossal growth of scientific collocations of atoms in the post modern society. Maugham's dialectical art in which man's basic instincts play a pivotal role in the making of the over all human consciousness—social, intellectual ethical, mystical and aesthetic, find a third space to define his self in the society at large. The dialectical art discerned by Maugham makes human consciousness to be a part of the collective psyche. Maugham believes that all the scientific, intellectual and evolutionary processes that take place at different levels of time, need to be readjusted with the aesthetic discipline of human life. Man would then no longer undergo the despair and pain of loneliness in the existing society. Eliot, in his remarkable essay, 'Tradition and Individual Talent' emphatically argues for infusing the historical sense for defining the form of a work of art. Maugham, on the other hand, is a disillusioned realist. To him bringing about human welfare and emancipation on the realistic plane, is no more feasible for carving a way out to emancipation of man. The scientific romance of H.G. Wells, no more remains romance as it stupefies man with all its enormity. Huxley in his Brave New World, explores all those iota of anguish that ironically inundates man from within. All the scientific revolutions brought about by man thus end with despair and dissipation. To Eliot, 'April is the cruelest month' ironically bring no spiritual awakening to man. W.B. Yeats yearns for living confined to his 'Ivory Tower'. Maugham thus shares the anguish of the modern age in which man ironically finds no space to aesthetically define the innate instincts which are themselves a larger reality. Thus from the dialectical art evolved by Maugham, emerges the whole being of man. Human aspirations for attaining emancipation says Maugham would then no more be trundled by the mechanistic order. Maugham is dialectically conscious of the factors which always remain at the back of substance of the human mind—act as a palatable force logistically reasoning to find a way out to the ingrained basic instincts which hold man in a state of bondage in the mechanical society.

Somerset Maugham's exploration of art, beauty and craftsmanship makes indelible imprint upon the human psyche. It would at the same time be uneven to limit Somerset Maugham to be merely a naturalistic writer; Maugham dialectically puts up rationale to probe the intricacies of human predicament taking into account the evolutionary and scientific progresses which man has so far achieved during his age-long-experience. Maugham with no less vigour evinces that the elemental and primitive and instinctual patterns too constitute the undercurrents of the streams of human consciousness and determine the shape of things to come in various syllogistic propositions. Maugham's dialectical art is thus an on-going process in which centuries long evolutionary processes taken up by Man to translate his dream of freedom into a concrete reality, is braced up with the dynamics of aesthetic sensibility.

Eliot on the one hand emphasizes to link up the 'historical sense' with the existing order to present a work of art. In Eliot's realm of criticism both 'tradition and individual talent' co-exist for presenting a complete picture of human life. Maugham on the other hand adroitly adopts a more realistic approach to the intricacies of the Post Modern Society in which Man is ironically oblivious of his own 'being'. As he is unconscious of the aesthetic and instinctual elements which constitute the mettle of the 'self', Man says Maugham, is a prisoner of his own illusory 'self'. Hence all the scientific, evolutionary and economic progresses heaped up in the post modern society says Maugham, are not the 'end of imagination'; instead the doctrine of the inner self which he braces up with the aesthetic emotion, itself standpoint, the dialectical approach to art and morality thus invents a more pragmatic vision in which the ever-growing human consciousness—Scientific, intellectual is linked up with the aesthetic discipline at different levels of time. Thus Maugham's anguish to make the invisible visible receives impetus to bring into focus all those factors that shape up the consciousness on the dialectical plane. Unlike Eliot Maugham doesn't argue for escaping from motley colours of the self. Poetry says Eliot is not the 'turning loose of emotions but escape from emotions.' 'Turning loose of emotions' for Maugham is tantamount to manoeuvering from the motley colours of the 'self'; ignoring the aesthetic emotion, to Maugham, is to escape from those inbuilt and ingrained 'emotions' which evoke a larger reality. As such Maugham presents a unified sensibility in which the discordant elements of science and religion do not fall apart instead they co-exist in complete harmony.

A dialectical approach to life is thus a 'summing-up' of all the scientific, evolutionary and humanistic processes braced up with aesthetic emotion in a bid to unfold the whole consciousness of the modern man. Thus Maugham's dialectical approach innovates a 'new scientific morality'. Man would then no longer feel himself alien in his own surroundings. Maugham envisions the need to look beyond the 'algebra of infinities'. The 'algebra of infinities' cropped up by the colossal growth of intellect says Maugham is devoid of catering to man's aesthetic aspiration in the post modern era. It can however be dialectically argued that the new scientific morality ironically inculcates man in alienation. Shaw, who was a disillusioned realist rationalistically argued for liberating society from shackles of idealism and illusion. Maugham on the other hand was of the view that the culmination of the 'real' world of which Shaw was a staunch exponent, is incompatible with the whole being of Man. Maugham hence dialectically argues that the colossal growth of science is not the end of imagination,; instead a re-integration of the 'real' and the aesthetic life can take man to the road of freedom and self-fulfilment.

Maugham's dialectical approach thus rationalises all the human endeavour applied to the evolutionary, scientific and technological planes in order to place man in the correct perspective.

Reference

1. Bertrand Russell; what I believe, p. 47.

Bibliography

W. Somerset Maugham; Heinemann/Octopus/Martin Seeker and Warburg, London, ed. 1979.

W. Somerset Maugham; The Moon and Six Pence, A Penguin International Edition, Penguin Books Ltd., Harmondsworth, ed., 1970.

W. Somerset Maugham; The Painted Veil, Penguin Books, ed., 1953

W. Somerset Maugham; Of Human Bondage, Random House, New York, ed., 1956

W. Somerset Maugham; Cakes And Ale, Penguin Books, ed., 1948.

W. Somerset Maugham; The Magician, Penguin Books, in Association with William Heinemann Ltd., ed., 1967.

W. Somerset Maugham; Catalina, Penguin Books, ed., 1967.

W. Somerset Maugham; The Summing up, Pocket Books, New York, ed., 1967.

W. Somerset Maugham; Collected Short Stories, Vol. Ill, Pan Books in association with William Heinemann, ed., 1976.

W. Somerset Maugham; Here and There, Melbourne, William Heinemann Ltd., ed., 1948.

W. Somerset Maugham; 'Of Heiman Bondage' (with digression on the art of fiction), An address by W. Somerset Maugham, Norwood Editions, 1978.

W. Somerset Maugham; "The Partial View, Heinemann Ltd., Melbourne, London, ed., 1954.

W. Somerset Maugham; "The Writer's Point of View", London, Published by the National Book League, The Cambridge University Press, ed., 1951.

W. Somerset Maugham; Great Novelists and their Novels, The John-C. Winston Company, Philadelphia, Toronto, ed., 1948.

W. Somerset Maugham; Creatures of Circumstances, The Sun Dial Press, Garden City, New York, ed., 1948.

W. Somerset Maugham; "Foreword", The Memoirs of Aga Khan, Classel and Company Ltd., London, 1954.

A. C. Bradley; Shakespearean Tragedy, Papermac, p. 52.

A Clutton Brock; "What is Art", Several Essays, Edited by G. F. Cumberledge, Oxford University Press, ed., 1952.

Aldous Huxley; Brave New World, Penguin Books, (In Association with Chatto and Windus), ed., 1966.

Anthony Curtis; 'Somerset Maugham', Weidenfield and Nicolson, London (Printed in Great Britain by Butter and Tanner Ltd.), Frome and London.

Arnold J. Toynbee; Greek Civilization and Character, A Mentor Book, (Published by the New American Library), ed., 1953.

Arnold Toynbee; Faith of a Historian, edited by K. M. Munshi and R. R. Diwaker, Bhartiya Vidya Bhawan, Bombay, ed., 1967.

Arnold Toynbee; Hellenism, edited by Gilbert Murray, Six George Clark, The Home University of Modern Knowledge, ed., 1958.

Arnold Bennet; The Old Wives Tale, Hodder and Stoughton, London; New York; Toronto.

Arthur Compton-Rickett; A History of English Literature, UBS Publishers' Distributors' Ltd. 1994.

Atkins John; Aldous Huxley : A Critical Study, Calder and Bouyars, London, ed., 1967.

B. Prasad; An Introduction to English Criticism, Macmillan India Ltd., Madras, Jaipur, Patna, ed., 1993.

Bertrand Russell; Mysticism and Logic, Unwin Books, London, ed., 1963. Bertrand Russell; Why I am not a Christian and other essays on religion and related subjects, edited by Paul Edwards, London, George Allen and Unwin Ltd., ed., 1964. Bertrand Russell; Marriage and Morals, Unwin Books, London, ed., 1970.

Bernard Shaw; Candida, Orient Longman, ed., 1994.

Bernard Shaw; Man and Superman, Surjeet Publications, New Delhi, ed., 1986.

B. G. Kuzentov; Philosophy of Optimism Progress Publishers, ed., 1977.

Bombert Victor; The Novels of Flaubert: A Study of Themes and Techniques, Princeton New Jeresy, Princeton University Press, ed., 1966.

Charles Dickens; David Copperfield, Rupa and Co. ed., 1990.

D. H. Lawrence; Women in Love, Avon Publications, Inc, New York, (First edition 1920, 1922, 1948, 1958).

D. H. Lawrence; The Lost Girl, Penguin Books in Association with William Heineman Ltd., ed., 1950.

D. H. Lawrence; Sons and Lovers, Penguin Books, ed., 1962.

Dorothy Parker, "The Portable", With an introduction by Somerset Maugham, New York, The Viking Press, ed., 1962.

D.H. Lawrence; The Letters of D.H. Lawrence, edited by Aldous Huxley, London William Heinemann, ed., 1932.

David Daiches, A Critical History of English Literature volume four, Rivised edition, Allied Publishers Limited, New Delhi, 1994.

E. M. Albert; T. C. Denise; S. P. Peter Freud; Great Traditions in Ethics, Eurasia Publishing House (P.) Ltd., New Delhi, ed., 1968.

Ebenstein William, Political Thought in Perspective, Mc-Grand Hill Book Company, Inc, New York, Toronto, London, ed., 1957.

E. M. Forster, Art for Art's sake, "The conscious reader, Caroline Shrades/Harry Fine Stone/Michael Shaugne, Macmillan, Publishing Co., Inc., New York, ed., 1974.

E. M. Forster; A Passage to India, Penguin Books, ed., 1979.

English Essays of To-Day, Published for the English Association by the Oxford University Press, London and New York, ed., 1954.

F. C. Copleston; Aquinas, Penguin Books Harmondsworth, Middlesex, ed., 1961.

Fei—Pai—Lu; T.S. Eliot: The Dialectical structure of his theory of poetry, University of Chicago, ed., 1966.

G. H. Mair, Modern English Literature, Oxford University Press, London, ed. 1956.

The Great American Thinkers Series, Henry David Thoreau, Washington Squire Press, Inc, New York, ed., 1968.

Gurko Leo; Joseph Conrad : Giant in Exile, Collier Books, Macmillan Publishing Co., Inc., New York, ed., 1979.

George Watson, The Literary Criticism Penguin Books, Harmondsworth, ed., 1964.

Honore De Balzac; "In the Desert", French Short Stories, Selected and Translated by R. G. Goodyear and P. Z. R. Wright, Jaico Publishing House, Bombay, ed., 1957.

Henry James, Portrait of the Lady, Modern Library College Editions.

Joseph Conrad, The Heart of Darkness Surjeet Publications, New Delhi, ed., 1988.

John Plamenatz, Man and Society, Longmans, Green and Co. Ltd., London, ed., 1963.

J. W. N. Sullivan; The limitations of Science, A mentor Book, Published by the New American Library, ed., 1963.

James Joyce, Portrait of the Artist as a Young Man, Penguin Books, ed., 1976.

J. C. Johari; Contemporary Political Theory, Sterling Publisher Private Limited, New Delhi, Bangalore, Jalandher, ed., 1985.

John Milton, Pradise Lost, (Book I), Published by Rajhans Prakashan Mandir, Meerut, ed., 1981.

Kalidasa; Sakuntala, Three Sanskrit Plays, Penguin Books Ltd., Harmondsworth, Middlesex England, ed., 1981.

Karl Jaspers, "is science Evil", "The conscious Reader,

Caroline Shrades/Harry Fine Stone/Michael Shaughne, Macmillian Publishing Co., Inc., New York, ed., 1974.

Kingsley Amis, I want it now, Panther Books Ltd., ed., 1969.

Lord Tennyson, In Memorium.

Leo Tolstoy; Annakarenina, Pan Books in Association with William Heinemann, ed., 1977.

Mathew Arnold, "on the modern element in Literature", Several Essays, edited by G.F. Cumberledge, Oxford University Press, ed., 1952.

Mathew Arnold, "The choice of subjects in Poetry," English Critical Essays; edited by Edmund Jones, Oxford University Press, Delhi, ed., 1971.

Martin Turnell, The Novel in France, Penguin Books, In Association with Hamssh Hamilton, ed., 1962.

Nirad C. Chaudhuri, A Passage to England, Orient Paperback, New Delhi.

Oscar Wilde; The Picture of Dorian Gray, Wordsworth Classics, Ed., 1993.

P. B. Shelley; Prometheus Unbound, Published by Arti Book Centre, Educational Publishers, New Delhi, ed., 1977.

P. G. Wode House, Preface to Uncle Fred; An Omnibus, Penguin Books, ed., 1991.

Paul Roubiczek; Existentialism for and against, London, Cambridge University Press, 1964.

The Pelican Guide to English Literature : The Modern Age, Vol. 7, A Penguin International Edition, ed., 1964.

Robert, G. Olson; An introduction to existentialism, Dover Publication, Inc., New York, ed., 1962.

Roshan Ara; Jasper's Concept of Freedom, The Aligarh Magazine, edited by S. Asim Ali, 1979-80. Aligarh Muslim University, Aligarh.

R. A. Scott - James, "Emancipation", The Making of Literature, Allied Publishers Pvt. Ltd., New Delhi, Bombay, Calcutta, ed., 1984.

Philip Lee Ralph , The Story of Our Civilization : A Study of the Western Peoples, ed., 1957.

Richard Aldington, W. Somerset Maugham, Double Day, Daren and Co., Inc., New York, ed., 1939.

Robert Frost, The Pocket Book of Frost's Poems, Pocket Books, Inc., New York, ed., 1946.

Susan Stontag, "The aesthetics of Silence" edited by William J. Handy and Max West Book, Light and Life Publishers, ed., 1974.

Several Essays, edited by G. F. J. Comburledge, Oxford University Press, ed., 1952.

S. H. Patil, A Text Book of Political Thought. (From Plato to Machiavelli) Vani Educational Books, A division of Vikas Publishing House Pvt. Ltd., New Delhi, ed., 1984.

Sarojini Naidu, Indian English Poetry, Orient Longman, ed., 1997.

T. S. Eliot, Selected Poems, Faber and Faber, London, Boston, ed., 1980.

T. S. Eliot; The Family Reunion, Oxford University Press, Bombay, Calcutta and Madras, ed. 1978.

T. S. Eliot; Tradition and Individual Talent.

Traub Stanley, Literacy Criticism of Oscar Wilde University of Nebraska Press, Lincoln, ed., 1976.

Thomas H. Huxley, Evolution and Ethics Macmillan and Co., United, St. Martin's Street, London, ed., 1925.

C

D

E

T

U

V

W

Y

Z